Doing Anything After Wo...

. . . What About Re...

A glimpse of things through the wrong end of life's telescope –

written, compiled, designed and produced by those of an uncertain age.

Doing Anything After Work? . . . What About Retirement?

Published by

Hucklow Publishing

for and on behalf of

©**Paul Bramley**

December 2009

ISBN: 978-0-9563473-1-2

Printed by
Hammer Design
Hathersage, Hope Valley
Derbyshire S32 1DP

Published and Distributed by:
Hucklow Publishing
Ash House
Great Hucklow
SK17 8RF

Tel: 01298 871385
peter.miles@hucklow.net

This book is dedicated to

those who don't know how to stop,

those who look for something special in retirement

and

those who feel that life has kicked them in the teeth.

In November 2008 the Minister for Women, Harriet Harman, announced that Dame Joan Bakewell had agreed to be "A Voice of Older People".

We are very delighted that she has written this Foreword.

Foreword

by Joan Bakewell

It always lifts my heart to hear of older people taking the initiative and passing on their wisdom and experience to others. This book just does that and deserves the success I am sure it will get. Being old has serious drawbacks, not least the loss of energy and resolve. Yet here is Hope Valley demonstrating how capable they are of getting their act together.

In more serious terms it has been shown that the arts and anything that demonstrates creativity is very good for the ageing brain. We are often exhorted to keep doing crosswords and solving puzzles but that's only the start. As we get older we have more time and more memories. Many of us want to pass on recollections and family histories to our grandchildren. Others want to warn of the hazards and pitfalls on not being as able as we once were. As this delightful book shows there is no end to the ways we can express ourselves. I am sure it will give many pleasures to a great range of people.

Do not grow old, no matter how long you live. Never cease to stand like curious children before the Great Mystery into which we were born. ~ *Albert Einstein*

Singing, fishing, meeting my close and dear friends, looking at pictures and nature, shocking a few people who deserve shocking, taking my pills, writing a book and swigging Irish Whiskey. These are my ways of fending off the old gent with the scythe waiting patiently to harvest me. ~ *George Melly*

Develop interest in life as you see it: in people, things, literature, music – the world is so rich, simply throbbing with treasures, beautiful souls and interesting people. Forget yourself. ~ *Henry Miller*

Enjoying sex, loving fashion, having fun, decorating our homes, going on lavish holidays – the list is endless. ~ *Joan Collins*

About this book

This, dear reader, is for you to browse and to enjoy. It certainly does not try to tell you how to live retirement nor have much to say about "growing old gracefully", especially the graceful bit.

It is a collection of loosely connected pieces by about forty individuals from a wide variety of backgrounds and experience. Their brief was to share experiences of retirement and associated ageing, to tell it as it is, from the heart and in their own style.

Some of the pieces are short and quirky, some serious, some angry, and some content. Others take a more biographical line and a few have more philosophical offerings. There is a leavening of humour and some swallow's flight of fancy. You will also find a sprinkling of light verse and a few fiercely sad poems.

The majority of contributors are either members of our local Probus club in the Hope Valley, Derbyshire, or their wives, plus a few friends who were interested and generous enough to contribute. Probus is a loose association of retired and semi-retired professional and business people throughout the United Kingdom.

Writers are listed on the acknowledgements page and are not identified with their articles. There are a few foreign imports to liven up the pages and where possible attribution is made, otherwise our friend Anon takes the credit.

The contributors are mostly in a stable financial situation, at least at the time of writing! They come from similar social backgrounds, but in spite of this they have produced widely different pieces in content, attitude and style.

'Quot homines tot sententiae' – so many men, so many opinions (Terence, 190-159BC)

Paul Bramley
December 2009

Freedom at last

Our official retirement age was 62 but I worked part time until I was 64. I was very keen to finish and do not miss work at all as it was quite stressful. May says she worried about retirement more than I did! She was convinced that I would get under her feet.

I do not like set routines so not setting an alarm clock and not having to go through the morning ritual five days a week was marvellous.

May and I have quite good health and do many things together. We are happy in each other's company. My great fear is that I may eventually be on my own. Luckily we have a daughter, son, two grand-daughters and a great grandson and we are a close-knit family.

I prefer physical pursuits i.e. gardening, walking, gymnasium but like to read the broadsheets and books of general nature and technical books but not novels.

I don't worry too much about myself but can get quite depressed about the world situation and its effect on the grandchildren.

To sum up – I have enjoyed very much the freedom that retirement gives you. I feel that there is no way that I would do my old job again.

Good health is the most important thing together with a good partner!

Retirement is?

A time of change.

A time for realising hopes and dreams of earlier years and a time to look forward and plan for the future.

A time when we can do what we want to do, not what others expect us to do.

A time of adjustment. Often two people who have had separate occupations find themselves together most of the time. They need individual space.

A time for putting into practice personal and social skills learnt in a lifetime of work.

A time spent with the grandchildren, a time for making new friends and renewing relationships with old ones.

A time for talking; time spent in pleasant conversation is never wasted.

A time for extra education in the form of mental, physical or social activities. A time to keep abreast of new technologies.

A time to belong to a group, a society, a church, fellowship or just a body of people who meet on a regular basis.

A time when time appears to be passing at an ever increasing pace.

A time when we recognize that we are slowing down both physically and mentally.

A time to show tolerance towards the ideas, aspirations and lifestyles of a younger generation.

A time to be aware of the frailties of the human body and, on occasions, its remarkable adaptations.

A time when illness or infirmity is more likely to occur. When it does, the effect can be a hiccup or can mean a complete change of lifestyle.

A time when two become one and we enter the unknown.

A nasty shock

Retirement has been a shock to our systems. Until you reach the age of 65, it is an age that belongs to your grandparents. Then suddenly you are faced with the irrefutable fact that anno domini applies to you as well. As William Shatner, of the Starship Enterprise, put it "The problem is that I've become an old guy. Me! An old guy! How did it happen? It must be a mistake!"

So now we try to ignore it and live as much as possible as if we were 45 instead of 65++. Working with young people helps a great deal. When one is with them the delusion kicks in and one forgets one's age – as long as nothing too strenuous is expected.

To our regret, we have found that it is important to have money. Without the 'readies' there is such a lot that cannot be done. Travel is restricted, diet tends to be affected, and thank goodness we don't smoke!

Ambitions fulfilled and goals achieved bring contentment and encouragement. The love of family and friends has been essential together with new plans for the future – new mountains to scale – challenges to beckon us on.

Perhaps health has been quite a big feature too, especially since the cancer operation and recovery. It makes you grateful for life and spurs you to live it to the full while you are still fit enough to do so.

Free swimming passes for the over 60s, well done Gordon – but where are they? If you don't hurry up, it will be too late!

What they did not tell me about retirement!

Dictionary Definition:

'Retire' – 'to stop or make someone stop working permanently, usually on reaching an age at which a pension can be received' or – 'to go away to rest, especially to go to bed!'

I am not sure `retirement' is the correct word – can you really retire at 53 years of age? It was more like a funded withdrawal from the work place. In my situation *they* only gave practical support like *managing your money*, *networking to find another position* and *doing consultancy work*. Six months *garden leave*, complete with company car concentrates the mind. How had my career come to a grinding halt seven years early?

The answers were in many ways blindingly obvious, but nevertheless difficult to accept because at no point up to being told was I ever aware that there was a plan for me to go at 53. (Having said that, so many colleagues were given similar treatment, some coping better than others.) What they didn't tell me was how to put my life back together after five years in a merged company of two companies which were so different that it was like mixing oil with water. Many people in this new company found themselves in negative equity, with company assisted mortgages, having moved from Sheffield to re-locate in London (not usually out of choice but to keep the job going and preserve a potential pension). Personal pressures were enormous.

'Retirement', when it came was a critical path procedure with very little personal contact (I only ever talked to close colleagues after I was put on garden leave – there was no business post, for example). So you tend to make decisions purely on your own judgement.

'What to do next?' How do I divest myself of the unpleasant baggage I have gained over the last five years? 'They' don't have any part in your well being. Like everything else in life it's basically 'Me, versus the rest of the world'. Having 'retired' for the first time, I emerged somewhat battered and damaged from five years in the newly merged company.

I knew I needed to take stock of my situation and rebuild myself from the psychological damage of the last few years. Plainly I was unable to replicate any of the jobs I had done earlier in my career, always assuming that such jobs were on offer. I knew I had to do something radically different; something that required less brain power but with enough interest to occupy the mind.

The first thing I did was to register with the local D.S.S. office. This turned out to be a cathartic experience, a great leveller! Typically, I was handed a long form to complete. Part of the form asked for my current hourly wage. Borrowing a calculator I arrived at a figure. The next question was 'What hourly rate would you settle for?' I knocked off 75% and then was told 'We haven't got any jobs paying that sort of money, luvvie!' I left the offices noticing a job paying £100 for a 60 hour week, I kept in touch with the D.S.S. who were endlessly helpful and pleasant.

I knew my previous company had money in the training budget. I applied to do two things:

1. Attend a residential Classic car restoration course.
2. Take an HGV licence.

I obtained the funding. I had one week on the restoration course in Church Stretton. I discovered I was the only one on the course! I learned as much about local hostelries as I did restoration but it was a great experience. My 'teacher' was a brilliant engineer who had recently built a replica Mk 1 Lola racing car which was, amazingly, street legal! He raced the car locally and I had a great time exploring the Shropshire roads around Church Stretton.

Back home I applied to enrol on an H.G.V. course at Darnall. A 6.30am start at the training centre concentrated the mind. However, after five and a half days I took the test and passed. Next problem – employment! 'Come back when you have some experience.' I got an eventual start via an agency. More work followed and then a full time job in Hope Valley. Quarries are an emotive subject. My sympathies are with the people working in the industry.

Hard work, early starts, low pay which barely covered my wine bill! One week later I concluded I had earned less than previous company expenses had generated, I learned a lot about what a struggle life was for many working people.

And then, gentle reader, things changed. I 'retired' again, only to emerge with an opportunity, which came out of the blue. A previous colleague had, after endless applications without a reply, got a position with a major company in the food industry. His job was in sales and our careers had in many ways mirrored each other.

He had progressed in the company and changes were being made. Their sales force was to be re-structured and they needed someone to do it. Wearing a suit for the first time in a long time I met the Managing Director and Sales Director and was offered a contract for two years. In essence my job description was to: -

- Reduce the sales force full time head count by 50% (i.e. make the other 50% redundant!)
- Recruit part time, typically female staff, to take up the slack.
- Train the remaining full time sales people to management standard.
- Keep happy five client companies (within the group) who used the sales force.
- Refine administration procedures.
- Introduce appraisal systems.
- Chair meetings, organise National Conferences etc.

The irony of reducing a Sales Force by 50% was not lost on me! The term 'Poachers and Gamekeepers' sprung to mind! I had mixed feelings about getting involved, but then I thought I would at least have sufficient understanding and empathy to be supportive. The company was part of a multinational. Basically it was a distribution company, onto which had been added a sales force. There was no sales management as such and distribution managers were trying to understand and run something that was alien to their culture.

I was given a budget and total power to 'get on with it'!! It was a superb challenge and I relished it, although found out later that two or three younger sales managers had declined the challenge! Then came four years where I came to terms with PCs for the first time, learned about 'hot desking' (first one into the office gets one!) and lots of other new issues. After a while I got to know one of the directors well and he confided in me that if I failed, he would go down with me! No pressure there then! He also told me that he didn't understand sales forces and wished me well!

The two years' contract became four and after this time I retired again. It still brings tears to my eyes when I recall that the sales force had a collection and presented me with a cut glass decanter that is still in use! The M.D. told me that he could not remember any managers ever having anything presented to them.

My retirement did not last long! I was now 60 and a young man nearby was building up a local garage business. His father-in-law lived next door and suggested a way of keeping fit. I did this for two or three years, building walls and mixing concrete and helping to build up the business. This was a good way to get myself finally retired!

Time to retire

I'm sorry to have been a little slow
It wasn't always thus. I'm sure you know
That in my prime I was quite quick
Never one to miss a trick
A jump ahead at every meeting
In there first with welcome greeting,
Winning points, remaining charming,
Healing wounds with smooth embalming.
I'm lucky now if I can hear
All that is said. It's not so clear.
First people mumble, then speak quickly,
My brain's like treacle, sticky, thickly,
Trying to find an apt reaction
But in fact I'm a distraction,
Boring, snoring, ranting on,
I think it's time that I was gone!

The spoons

I found the spoons again today,
Muddled with the forks and knives,
Amid the debris of our lives.
I hide the mirror when it lies.
Where is the girl with laughing eyes?
And not that haggard wreck who cries.
And who are you ? You seem to care.
You hold my hand and stroke my hair,
But in your eyes I see despair.

Carved ivory Memento Mori, pendants to a Rosary

Childhood

My happy child, Why smile at me?
What is our future that you see ?
My darling child, Oh not that pain,
In age to be a child again.
Are you that child, who sick with care
Will seal my lips, untwist my hair,
And close my eyes you cannot bear
When from the edge of life I stare.
And will our love which now we share
Turn to that hatred of despair
And will I be your cross of pain
When age becomes a child again ?
My happy child why smile at me
If this our future that you see ?

Banners of dawn

With gratitude to the writings of Siegfried Sassoon and
part of this poem which I have cherished for years:

> *Return to me colours that were my joy*
> *Not in the woeful crimson of men slain*
> *But shining as a garden, come with the streaming*
> *Banners of dawn, and sundown after rain . . .*

(From "Victory" published anonymously in
the Times on January 15, 1916)

So you're right down the pile where you started,
Trained, qualified, and unemployed.
Older, and wiser?
Or just thinking less clearly,
Is it new life or a void?

The gifts and farewells were so touching,
They'll miss you, and, doubtless, you them;
Whereas those few
Whose frosty hello
And ways they looked through you
Can go.

But, there's birdsong and sun in the garden
A child's laughing joy in the air,
Loved ones that you meet
A cat at your feet
Brings joy, but despair.

Our paths are clouded and twisting,
Our goalposts, so sure, now are gone;
Yet some days it's so clear,
There's so much to do,
While on others . . .
                    . . . just fear.
But we're here!

I can do it myself

One of my daughters' first words were not "Mummy" or "Daddy" but "I can do it myself" - or at least that's my memory.

Starting into retirement was much the same for me. Now I had the time; I have used the skills over the years and so why not do the gardening, the decorating, the car maintenance, the tax returns, electrical repairs, clear the gutters, . . . and continue helping other members of the family with all the above - and more.

Day 1 – I am going to decorate the dining room.

Day 2 – I am not going to tackle the height of the hall, stairs and landing.

Day 3 – Enrolled at college on a Cabinet Making course.

Day 4 – My ladder is 15 years old. Maybe the rungs are not so secure. Chop it up and find someone else to clear the gutters.

Day 5 – Joined a local choir.

Day 6 – Joined a reading group.

Day 7 – Regrouped the hi-fi and television set-up.

Day 8 – Joined a rambling group.

Day 9 – Looked at the wiring to a kitchen fitting. New regulations mean that I must employ a qualified electrician. Frustration.

Day 10 – Bought a new computer. What a difference having access to broadband.

Day 11 – Joined an Alexander Technique course at the local college.

Day 12 – Am I filling up my life too much?

Day 13 – What don't I want to spend time on?   Get a tax consultant to complete my annual tax return.

Day 14 – WOW - This is much better than being tied to a working schedule –but I need to consider what I do want to spend time on.

Every day is a chance to review the present and also to consider future possibilities.

Early days and early questions

It is August 2008, I am sixty-nine years old and I retired fifteen months ago. People ask: "Are you enjoying your retirement?" My stock reply is that my wife and I have spent the last fifteen months selling our old house, buying a new one and altering it so that we can live in it. I have not had time to be retired.

I have not been to any seminars on retirement. I have not had counselling. Well not yet. My retirement has so far been a DIY job. But how am I going to deal with this radical change in my life? How am I going to deal with the equally radical change in my relationship with my wife? How am I going to ensure that we both keep as mentally and physically fit as possible and stave off the inevitable decline for as long as we can? I am terrified of drift, of getting to the end of the third year of retirement and finding that all I have done is read a few detective stories, watched too many videos and gone for a few walks.

My children have asked me what I am going to do in my retirement. What is my strategy for the next decade or so? Some of my friends who retired shortly before I did have recommended that I prepare a written list of the things I want to do. A list of projects, this advice makes sense. I must have something to make me get out of bed at half past seven in the morning, wash, shave and dress. I must not get into bad habits, become lazy and scruffy and I must not in any circumstances trespass on my wife's domain. So I started to prepare a mental list. I hit a problem; nearly all the items on my list of projects and activities were what I wanted to do with me. I have a wife and we want to do some things together. Oh yes, I forgot; she may have a list as well. There is another factor; I have assumed that we

will both be in excellent health. The preparation of the list or lists with health options and a timetable has been postponed. Let's get the house sorted and then I will really get down to being retired. Am I making excuses? Am I running away from the problem? Am I waiting for Godot? Probably.

I am glad that I retired. I was getting tired and I was beginning to miss points. Do I miss the work? I don't think so. What I miss is that every working day and sometimes on Saturdays and Sundays I went to an office and there would be piles of files on my desk and on the floor awaiting attention, with problems to solve, letters to dictate, telephone calls to make and people to meet. I miss the challenges, the little grey cells hurtling around at a hundred miles an hour and the adrenalin pumping.

I am ashamed of the mistakes I made and they haunt me. I must learn to put them down. I am proud of some of the things I have done during my life and sometimes think: Gosh, I did that!

An awakening

I dream very little
By days or by nights
In fact I am quite jealous
Of minds which take such flights
I have a friend who lost her man
The same year end as me
And she dreamed of him constantly
Her joy was plain to see
She'd relay all the detail
Just normal situations
Tho' some sounded quite far-fetched
Perhaps her dream creations
I thought I might compete
And fabricate a dream
Of something I'd enjoyed
Somewhere we had been
But before this was perfected
And ready for the telling
I had a dream for real one night
Of substance quite compelling
John used to do the man tasks
In the garden and you'd see
Him chop down trees and cut the grass
– After – some such fell to me
I'm not good with machinery
But mastered the ride-on mower
After one or two small crashes
And scratching the barn door
So I had this dream
I was cutting down the drive
And quarrelled with a conifer
And nearly took a dive.
We'd had some heavy showers
Front wheel caught in mud and muck
I tried reverse manoeuvre

But was well and truly stuck
Suddenly dear John appeared
All casual and smiling
Said 'Oh dear, what a cock-up!'
In soft tones quite beguiling.
He just pushed the machine
It slid gently back
He disappeared, I carried on
And finished off the track

What is really strange
I swear there's now a mark
On the dreamed-of conifer
A stretch of damaged bark
This reminds me of his coming
And to take more care
I don't think I need dreams
I know he's here and there . . . !

V. Jean Tyler in *Survival! A book of Everyday Verse*

Life curls round a downward spiral: learning, working and retiral: filling time and then "expiral"

I often ask myself the question "What is life all about?" My mother used to tell me that our sole purpose is to prolong life and that having descendants was the true meaning of eternal life. There is no doubt that I have fulfilled her interpretation having had two children and five grandchildren. However, loving and caring for my husband and family, whilst occupying my life from birth to eventual death, has not been the whole of my life. I have no doubt that the characteristics which have influenced how I lead and have led my journey to date have pervaded both my personal and working life but I am also in no doubt that there have been two distinct individuals in evidence: "myself" and my "alter ego", who was the working woman.

Retirement has often been likened to bereavement in the impact it has on our lives. For me it was a bereavement in that my alter ego was instantly lost. I mourned the loss of a life which fulfilled me and stretched my abilities to the limit. My education and experience was put to good use and expanded throughout my working life. I was valued for my performance and recognised as an individual in an environment totally divorced from my personal life. A high level of responsibility for the development and training of a significant number of people and for the expansion of the company for which I worked gave me great satisfaction and constant challenges.

Then it ended.

The "myself" part of me carried on as before: wife, daughter, sister, mother, grandmother, niece, aunt, and friend. Make no mistake, this part of my life is wonderful. There is no substitute for a loving family and we all know how time consuming and rewarding it can be. How thankful I am for a retirement which allows me so much more time for all those activities I love, not least travelling. How sad I am for those people who, like my father, died before retirement. He came from a poor beginning and worked hard to get out of it only to die before the enjoyment of time for himself and his family.

I have been fortunate to have been able to have a good, fulfilling working life and an enormously satisfying personal life but I do feel as if I have been two distinct people, one of whom has gone. I also know, however, that for many, many people, retirement is nothing but a happy release from hard, soul destroying work which gives no satisfaction other than a pay packet. For those who make it to retirement, the joy of free time can be enormous, finance and purpose permitting.

I think retirement means so many different things to different people and there can be no real advice to those about to reach that age. So many factors come to play on an individual's view. Enough finance to keep the wolf from the door, someone with whom retirement can be shared and enjoyed, good health – something which becomes more difficult with advancing years, interests to keep one's mind alive – all have a part to play in filling the retirement years.

There is no doubt that one of the most disturbing things about retirement is that there is an enormous pool of skill and experience which is lost to the country. Over 65s make up 16% (around 9.6 million) of the population. The top end of the workforce must give way to youth but is it sensible to lose such talent? Perhaps the ageing process makes it inevitable and no matter how able one feels inside, failing fitness and health could interfere with continuation in work. There is a dreadful new word "returnment" which means a return to work after retirement and for many this has become a reality and a necessity.

I am reminded that my husband practised "returnment" and retired a number of times only to be drawn back into work on many occasions because of his expertise. He finally retired in the year 2000 declaring that he was not millennium compatible and did not look back. Perhaps it was a recognition that time moves on apace and finally he was not prepared to move with it at the same speed. The truth is retirement has given him a chance to develop in areas for which he had no time previously – golf and computer technology, for instance. Indeed, both he and I now teach computer skills to friends and neighbours and constantly "troubleshoot". So, whilst no longer in the rat race, we still make use of our knowledge.

Just as a last thought, the dictionary definition of retirement shows us that:

to retire can mean to leave office or employment, to withdraw, go away, retreat, or go to bed.

Oh dear!

A heart attack

I wouldn't much like to go
through it again
it causes such trouble
- and then there's the pain.
Riding along on
the Northern line
back from the theatre
everything's fine
when out of the blue
you're fighting for air
and you can't understand
the pain that is there.
You need some help
you look around
but at that time of night
on the Underground
they look away
don't know what to do,
you feel so glad
you're with someone like Sue.
Grit your teeth
and hope for the best,
it will soon go away
this pain in the chest.
It's spreading up
it's getting much worse
you close your eyes
and utter a curse,
I must get out
put an end to this ride
Sue's come over
she's now by my side.
Oh what a ghastly situation
struggling out of
Chalk Farm station,
the ambulance comes
they do their stuff

"Hold on governor
we know it's tough
we're taking you straight
to the A & E
just down the road
at the Royal Free".
They phone ahead
while we are dashing,
siren wailing
and blue lights flashing.
We lurch round a corner
on with the brakes
we're here at last,
but for heaven's sakes
I hope they're not busy
can get on with me quick,
I don't think I've ever
been quite so sick,
I'll compose myself
regain my poise
try to keep calm
not make so much noise.
Surrounded by doctors
and nurses as well
they quickly find out
what is giving me hell
a jab in the arm
an enzyme infusion
diamorphine by vein
brings the pain
to conclusion.
Consciousness slips
a warm pleasant feeling
sleepy and drowsy
I think I am healing,
an oxygen mask
is over my face

I hope the elastic
will keep it in place!
Now I'm awake
in a room in a bed
with Sue at my side
she's stroking my head
the pain's coming back
even worse than before
I have more diamorphine
more and yet more.
"I'll continue with this
again and again
until you are fully
relieved of your pain".
Looking straight in my eyes
so said the night sister
an angel of mercy
I just could have kissed her.
With her on my left side
and Sue on my right
Sue prayed, and I hoped,
that I'd get through the night,
but I thought that my heart
had a second attack
and was failing me now
and I'd never get back.
The pain is fading
it isn't so bad
I seem to be floating,
what a good life I've had,
my breathing is shallow
I can't keep awake
if this is the end
it's not a mistake,
Sue's here with me now
and it doesn't feel bad,
thank you Lord

for the life that I've had.
I am waking up
in that very same bed,
Sue's right beside me
she's stroking my head
the drips are both flowing
the monitors bleep
I'm alive and still going
I've just been to sleep,
the sun through the window
brings a new day
I open my mouth
and I hear myself say
"Will someone go out please
and find the car
it's at Brent Cross station
and not very far
from the A41
it's parked on the right
it shouldn't be left there
all day and all night".
Within a week
I had no more fears
I could walk about
and climb the stairs,
they sent me home
to recuperate,
and here we are
we've enough on our plate
rebuilding our lives
with the help of our friends,
eternally glad
that love never ends.
I wouldn't much like
to go through that again
it causes such trouble,
− not to mention the pain.

The poem opposite was written in 1997 soon after recovering from a heart attack. In 2001 his wife Sue also had a serious heart attack. Ry writes as follows:

"I was devastated and she was saved in the nick of time by an emergency balloon angioplasty. There was a surgical team on standby to do an emergency by-pass. I had to sign the consent form as Sue was incapable. She was stuffed full of thrombolytic, enzymic drugs. I could not see how she could survive.

The trauma I experienced coping with Sue's near death experience was the worst time of my life. Similarly it was for her, when she stayed up all night at my bedside in the Royal Free in 1997. It was devastating for her yet she and I, after the diamorphine, remember nothing of the critical events which followed and remained euphoric for several days."

The message is clear. It is the loving partner who suffers far more than the patient at the time of a medical emergency.

Forced retirement and the end of a school

The circumstances of my retirement were very painful for me. I was sixty two and knew that I would have to retire at sixty five and in fact was looking forward to a change of pace and being able to indulge my interests but I had not expected to be summarily dismissed as if my twenty three years of service counted for nothing.

After several years out of teaching while I looked after my children I had been extremely fortunate to be offered a teaching post relatively near to home in my specialist subjects of Latin and Greek which were even then fast disappearing from the curriculum and I was even more fortunate to be allowed to continue teaching my subject into my sixties. Not many Classics teachers of my generation have had that privilege. Not only was I able to be an advocate for the Classical world and its relevance for today's students but I liked the ethos of the school. It was a small school by today's standards which meant that the staff could know the students well and be concerned for their individual welfare especially since many of the students were boarders with families in far flung parts of the world. Moreover there was a prevailing atmosphere of respect and cooperation between the staff and a determination to work for the school's survival in an increasingly competitive environment.

Once my own children became more independent I became Director of Studies with the added responsibility for publicity and promotion of the school as well as being Head of Classics. I worked long hours, often I am afraid to the detriment of my family, but along with my colleagues, I felt that what the school offered its students was worth trying to preserve and promote. In spite of my age I had received a 'very good' grade in the recent inspection which had convinced me that I still had something to offer.

I had worked for two Heads, both of whom I had trusted and respected but on the retirement of the second my nemesis struck. It was unfortunate that the Head, the Deputy Head and the Bursar all retired within a year of each other leaving me as almost the longest serving member of staff. The staff had their misgivings about the newly appointed Head which in the event proved justified. Two weeks after her arrival at the beginning of the summer term the new Head informed me that she had no further work for me in the following term. There was no discussion or explanation. She had assumed that my contract had terminated when I was sixty whereas it ran until I was sixty five years old and I presume she thought I was an easy target. I was the first of several to be told their services were no longer required which kept the Unions busy and cost the Governors of the school many thousands of pounds. The atmosphere in the staff room became one of panic. Who was to be next? All trust had gone.

The parents and students were not informed that I was leaving at the end of term without a replacement and that all Classics courses would cease including GCSE and A Level. My Union had advised me that it was not for me to tell the parents or students that I had been dismissed but at a parents' evening in the last week of term, I thought I could not let parents assume that their daughters' courses were continuing. As a result I was blamed by the Head for the parents' understandable anger. She forbade the students and staff to give me an official leaving present and I was denied the customary valediction – after twenty three years of commitment to the school and its students. I felt I was being kicked out of the back door of the very school to which I had become so attached and for which I had worked so hard.

I was not surprised that I had been dismissed since I realised there was little room on the timetable for Latin but I had hoped that the popular subject of Classical Civilisation might have been preserved. With this end in view I had volunteered the previous year, when the new Deputy Head had been appointed, to give up most of my responsibilities and work only three days a week. It was clear, however, that the new Head wanted me out of the way and any discussion about further reduction of hours was useless even though it would have saved the governors from paying out for my redundancy. To be fair I could not contemplate continuing to work for a Head who had so little respect for her staff. It was the way the Head had spoken to me and her refusal to acknowledge any contribution I might have made to the school that upset me personally, but what I saw happening to the school generally, the threats to some of my colleagues, the fear and sense of helplessness which gripped the staff and the sudden disintegration of a happy, friendly and trusting community which made me so very angry. There was the added fear that the school could soon be in financial trouble; simple maths told us that the income derived from the number of pupils at that time could not cover the apparent spending spree on which the Head had embarked.

I cannot deny, though, that I was also very hurt that, at the end of a long career in teaching, I had had no official recognition of my work, although my colleagues did give me a farewell party away from the school premises and I still treasure the present they gave me of a tree for my garden.

It was only at the beginning of the next term that the full realisation hit me of what it meant to be plunged into retirement. My colleagues were in almost daily touch with me updating me on the latest disaster and asking for my advice. It was clear the school was on a downward spiral with parents beginning to withdraw their children. In retrospect this close contact made it difficult to disassociate myself from the gradual collapse of the school and the fates of my colleagues and our students. My life seemed very empty, there was no structure or apparent purpose to it apart from looking after my husband and he was very capable of doing this for himself. In fact he was looking after me since I had become quite depressed and suffered from innumerable migraines.

The worst of my depression lasted for about a year but my husband says it took two years for me to fully emerge from it. I can remember crying a lot and feeling so ill from the terrible migraines. I felt I had been foolish to devote so much of my energy, often at the expense of my family, for so many years to a school which it now seemed would inevitably close and whose Governors, it appeared, had rejected me out of hand. I did not regret the time I had spent actually teaching the students – that I had really enjoyed, but I was angry with myself for devoting so much extra energy to the organisation and promotion of the school; time and energy which it seemed could have been better spent. I could not understand why the Governors, many of whom I had come to know personally through serving on their board as staff representative for several years, appeared to have acquiesced in the manner of my dismissal

The Governors seemed to have been in denial of what was really happening in spite of many attempts to tell them. I have since discovered that they were oblivious of the real situation until it was too late and the many letters written in protest to the Chairman had not been revealed to them. It took eighteen months and the withdrawal of many of the students for the Governors to realise finally their mistake and for the head's contract to be terminated. When they discovered the size of the debt which had accrued during her headship the Governors were advised to put the school into administration from which it never recovered. The school changed hands twice and the business was finally declared bankrupt. And so the school which was reputed to be one of the oldest girls' schools in England closed.

Once the school was irrevocably closed it was easier to move on and accept that that part of my life was over. My husband was very patient and encouraged me to divert my energy to other interests. I set about restructuring our extensive garden which gave me both a sense of achievement and peace. I became more involved in the life of our church and joined various committees, becoming chairman of our village committee which absorbed much of my energy and helped me to become much more integrated into the community.

At last I was able to give more time to my family, enjoy visiting my children and, as grandchildren were born, delight in helping to look after them. This above all has given me the greatest sense of fulfilment and still does.

I had always had an interest in pottery but never had time previously to try to create any pots myself. I joined an evening class and then enrolled as a very mature student at Derby University on their part time Ceramics course which leads to a Higher Diploma. Sadly I am about to embark on the final module and I shall miss the stimulation of working with my fellow students. The course which started with learning to throw on a wheel and then developed through all aspects of decoration and firing proved to be quite inspirational and I feel very privileged to have been introduced to the work of many famous potters. Although I will never join their ranks I have taken over most of my husband's workshop to house my wheel and kiln and to create my own workspace, (he does have four other sheds and a garage!) and I continue to gain great pleasure from experimenting and trying to create a satisfying pot.

Latterly much of my time has been absorbed in managing a project for which the village was awarded a grant from the Heritage Lottery Fund. The aim has been to research and record the history of lead mining in and around the village by producing a book, setting up a lead trail with interpretation boards and compiling a village archive. I have found the research engrossing and the more I discover about the history of the people of the area the more I have gained a profound sense of what we owe to the past and feel an increased affinity with the place.

Gradually my life as a teacher has become part of history too and I can remember the good times without dwelling on the circumstances of my retirement. It is almost as if I have erased that painful episode of my life from my mind until I am asked to recall it. At seventy I am only too aware that there is still so much to do and enjoy. I still have my health and am fit enough to take great pleasure from long walks with my husband. I have the leisure to indulge my interests and above all enjoy the company of family and friends.

When I was first asked to write this piece a year ago I was surprised and overwhelmed by my emotional response to my dismissal even after seven years. I wrote a piece full of self-pity and bitter anger and am embarrassed to read it now. However, the very act of pouring out my emotions on paper, or rather computer, seems to have acted as a purge and I can now reflect on that period of my life in a more balanced way. I acknowledge that I was fortunate to be dismissed when I was, since I avoided the traumas of the following two years which many of my colleague had to endure. Moreover, in the current climate of redundancies I have little to complain about. It is a sobering thought that there are many thousands who must be facing the pain of redundancy and most of them without the security of a pension.

Another person declared redundant

WOLSEY:

Farewell! a long farewell, to all my greatness!
This is the state of man: to-day he puts forth
The tender leaves of hopes; to-morrow blossoms,
And bears his blushing honours thick upon him;
The third day comes a frost, a killing frost;
And, when he thinks, good easy man, full surely
His greatness is a-ripening, nips his root,
And then he falls, as I do. I have ventur'd,
Like little wanton boys that swim on bladders,
This many summers in a sea of glory,
But far beyond my depth: my high-blown pride
At length broke under me, and now has left me,
Weary and old with service, to the mercy
Of a rude stream, that must for ever hide me.
Vain pomp and glory of this world, I hate ye:
I feel my heart new open'd. O! how wretched
Is that poor man that hangs on princes' favours!
There is, betwixt that smile we would aspire to,
That sweet aspect of princes, and their ruin,
More pangs and fears than wars or women have;
And when he falls, he falls like Lucifer,
Never to hope again.

William Shakespeare, *Henry VIII*, Act III, Scene II

Did I fall or was I pushed?

It has happened to many before and will happen to many after. Why then does one feel so isolated, so alone and so defensive after it occurs?

I am talking about something with many titles . . . the sack, redundancy, resignation, departure by mutual agreement, leaving through ill health, has found another position and so on.

The circumstances of its occurrence have many variants. Closure of a business, relocation of an operation, take over, merging of companies, politics, differences of opinion, one simply just doesn't fit – you never know the true reason, although one is found. There are many other reasons besides.

It can occur suddenly without any indication and be a shock. It can follow a long period of rumour and innuendo and come almost as a relief. It can occur properly (if such a thing is possible) after proper discussion and consultation and when one's departure is truly by mutual consent. Whatever the circumstances, the higher you are, the harder you fall, but you all end up in the same place.

The numbness and emptiness of mind interchange with periods of anger, of calm and, most encouragingly, long periods of planning and logical thinking about what the future holds for you and yours.

My departure, at 52 years of age, came about because of a change of Chairman of the group in which I worked as MD of a large business. In the simplest terms, I could not develop any respect for him, personally or professionally.

In the knowledge that the policies being adopted and against which I had fought hard would threaten the people within the business, I set about doing all that was possible to minimise the impact of the future upon them.

After many months the great day of reckoning came and very civilised it was too, with little or no acrimony. The Chairman did not feel that I would act in the best interests of the company through its disposal and would be too protective of its employees. I was asked to approve of my replacement and to continue to run the business for a further six months. In return I would accrue further benefits, financial and otherwise, would be given counselling and advisory assistance and the most generous severance package. My departure would be "to move on to another job" assisted by one of the top headhunting companies in the UK at that time, and its true nature kept from the business, i.e. a prelude to disposal.

Here was the first spoke in the works: I did not want another job! I had always planned to retire at 55 years of age, to potter productively in a non-stressful way for a further 5 years or so, living mainly off my final salary scheme pension fund and the income from other investments. No one around me (except for my wife and family) knew that was so. I was "all right Jack". Why then was it a stressful situation?

Disposal would, because of inevitable subsequent rationalisation, threaten the future of many people who had shown much loyalty to me and to the company. I quickly resolved to take actions regarding the administration operations (which would undoubtedly be shut down) and the five manufacturing units scattered throughout the UK (two of which would be at considerable risk); actions, which might give some advantage to individuals and to groups of people when their day of reckoning came. I felt no loyalty was necessary to my "lords and masters" in taking such actions.

My subordinates were totally taken aback by many of my actions and I consoled myself by knowing that all would become clear to them in the not-too-distant future. My main board colleagues were too pre-occupied with planning "the exciting future ahead" to notice what was going on in the company I controlled.

So I played the games. I enrolled with prestigious headhunters and went for interviews with companies seeking experienced people such as myself. Or were they? I constantly felt my age (52) was a barrier as was the fact that I had worked for the same company for over 25 years. It gave me enormous satisfaction subsequently to point out to the headhunters the deficiencies of the company concerned and why I would never contemplate joining them (phrased in the nicest possible way, of course).

I attended the counselling courses to prepare me for coping with the trauma of redundancy, and for the changed world I faced if I retired. Both were formal and organised statements of the obvious. The only thing I recall as being of any value was the advice that when you are no longer an MD, people will cease to answer the 'phone straight away or to return your call very quickly. It saved much frustration.

Through all of this I continued my negotiations for my severance package and I much enjoyed exposing my colleagues to the degree of skill I had established in negotiations. All those years of pain with Tesco, Sainsbury, ASDA et al, not to mention the various unions, was to be alleviated by the package I negotiated for myself and mine.

I knew I had done everything possible for the people I would be leaving behind and, when I drove out of the gates of the business for the last time (in the nearly new former company car now belonging to myself) I felt only joy, even though I had no idea of what lay ahead.

How does one describe the shedding of stress? Whilst engaged in the boiling pot of the commercial world you are totally unaware of stress as such. It had sometimes risen to the surface and, after medical investigation, it was a relief to be told that when the symptoms appeared one should breathe into a brown paper bag. And it worked, albeit causing some expressions of surprise amongst others – "is he really breathing into a bag?"

After a short time you wake up without a million thoughts zinging through your brain, think only about walking the dog, what you might have for breakfast and, eventually, what the day holds for you. No train or plane to catch, no long drive ahead, no notes to scan for the first meetings of the day. Just calm, and a relaxing first cup of coffee drunk leisurely, not slurped on the run.

You feel some kind of guilt at feeling so good, at not feeling the intensity previously engendered when engaged in any project. No politics of course (as in "what does he really mean when he says that?") or the heavy weight of the knowledge your actions might have on thousands of employees.

You can meet up with family and friends more often, reward yourselves with holidays, both short breaks and great adventures, go to the theatre and sporting events without having to be responsible for guests or colleagues, or simply put on your boots and wander off into the countryside with your thermos and your binoculars.

A whole new non-stressful world emerges and you wonder how in heaven's name you had actually convinced yourself you enjoyed working!

Because of my business experience, I was invited to join in purchasing and developing a small specialist headhunting firm. It cost us two pounds and for that we took on its staff, debts and past records.

As a non-executive director, I had enormous satisfaction for the next five years in helping the business to establish a firm base and then to develop it into a highly successful enterprise.

Fifteen years later it continues to flourish. I now moved into total retirement.

An initial consultancy, albeit a tongue in cheek venture, plus the involvement in the headhunting business, had been a very valuable transitional period.

As we entered the millennium year the picture was clear. We had many hobbies; we travelled a great deal, spent a lot of time with family and friends and engaged in active sports such as shooting, bowls, short tennis and badminton. Our time was full. Everything was affordable, we lived within our income but capital items such as cars came out of investments, as did big and costly adventures.

You mean my wife had another life?

At the time of my 'falling or being pushed' our children had settled marriages (and still have) and our fourth grandchild had just been born, the eldest being four years old.

The two families lived 40 miles and 200 miles away respectively. Our son and son-in-law were in professional positions in progressive companies: one in the financial service industry and the other in manufacturing. They were the main providers. We wanted to give (in addition to the love and advice inherent within any balanced family) a discreet and balanced material assistance at a time when they were both under financial pressure. We already had a clear picture of the implications of inheritance tax as it was structured at that time, and that knowledge strongly influenced our thinking.

Apart from local friendships, we had a number of long term friendships maintained since our youth or forged over the previous decade.

Retirement was the opportunity for us, together, to see a great deal more of family and friends than had previously been the case, but we had no structured thoughts as to how we might do this.

My wife had developed interests in the WI, had taken adult education opportunities, was set upon improving her computer skills and had developed her own separate group of friends through those interests.

Outside of game shooting, I had no interests outside of my work other than reading, gardening, walking in the countryside and our dog.

Those are my recollections of the situation at my retirement from full-time employment. What were my wife's recollections and thoughts at that time?

Wife's Thoughts:

Never having kept a diary (only appointments diary) as my husband has, I really was quite nonplussed when I saw the insert "Wife's Thoughts". What were my thoughts then? It seems a lifetime away!

I suppose the first one was of relief. I had seen the strain of trying to keep a very large business going in an unfavourable economic climate take its toll on him. Relaxation techniques that I had learnt at one of my "keep-fit" classes proved useful when he was finding it difficult to sleep.

I was not worried about financial matters, as I knew we would be well provided for and we had never "over-extended" ourselves. No big mortgage for us! We wanted to be in the position for my husband to be able to walk away at any time he felt the pressures too much.

I was totally unprepared, as most wives approaching their husbands' retirement, for having him home with me all the time. He was about to gain his freedom, was I about to lose some of mine?

Would I miss the glamorous social life we were used to? Would I miss the perks we had become used to? Possibly. However, I had my three lovely grandchildren and one about to be born. In many ways, this was about to become one of the happiest periods of my life.

. . . . So, we are at August in my first weeks of retirement. This was marked by a most unusual occurrence. Whilst relieving myself in the woods, my dog disturbed a wasps' nest in the vicinity and one of them chose to show its annoyance by stinging the nearest bare flesh it could find. It was a clear lesson that I was mortal, especially when much swelling (of an abnormal nature) took place.

comments regarding inheritance tax and to our desire to share our good fortune with our families when they needed it most.

They had no problem with the knowledge of our desire to not unduly influence their lives by such actions, but that we wanted to do so whilst we could enjoy the short and long-term benefits to them of our "investment in their future".

Ties with my old company were finally severed completely and we moved into my first full year of retirement.

Those are my perceptions but what did "the lady of the house" think?

My diary records my enjoyment of the first months of "freedom" with short breaks, countryside pursuits, family and the garden at the forefront.

Towards the end of the year, my daughter became very concerned at the number of times the entry "fed up" appeared in my diary and was much relieved to learn it was my record of going to the local farm to feed our pheasant stock prior to the shooting season.

What was she doing reading my diary? It had always been an "open book" for the family – a practise developed in my working days as they sought gaps in my busy schedule to arrange visits or social events.

We made an early decision following retirement and the substantial monies we had been fortunate to accumulate (not least through my severance package) to share financial information completely and openly with our family. This locked into earlier

Wife's Comments:

At that time I was taking a computer course at a newly converted local business centre. Many women applied but there were only 10 places to be filled and I gained one of them. And so the tables were turned. Off I trotted each morning with my brief case after waving goodbye to my husband, knowing that I would have a meal cooked for me when I returned home. He would make a very good house-husband but needs a little more care when hoovering!

This course became an eye-opener for me. It would take a year and I would forge some very good friendships along the way. In many ways it eased our way into retirement, as we were not locked together every day – something I hear many wives complain about. "If only he would let me go shopping on my own" is a plaintive cry I have often heard.

. . . . So, we had taken a breather. There was a lot to be done!

The Head Hunting business – its purchase, re-location, re-training, recruitment of staff and business development plans took a lot of time in the initial period following its purchase.

We found time for one first big adventure – my retirement reward – following an England cricket tour in the West Indies; images that will never be forgotten, both of the countries and their people, but also for the cricket.

Now that "social" shooting had reduced substantially (the business connections had largely been lost) I concentrated on developing my hobby by greater involvement in a small local shoot on the estate of a working farm in the area.

Building pens, managing woodland, clearing bracken, mending stone walls, rearing the birds, controlling predators, I displayed manual skills lost in time and my knowledge of the countryside improved by leaps and bounds. Can you imagine calling in stoats (that had been killing our pheasants) by imitating their calls and succeeding in shooting them? I was eventually to shoot my first fox on these grounds, having previously taken part in fox "drives" through the local valley. No horses and hounds here, just men and dogs.

Family and friends increasingly occupied more of our time; time restricted by the need to talk to solicitors, financial and tax advisors and to make important decisions as to the wise investment of our funds.

Throughout all this came my first awareness of the life my wife had created. There were actually times when she could not make (or would not make) dates I had agreed. "So tell the WI you cannot make it," said I. "Get stuffed" said she, or something similar in woman talk.

My diary showed entries along the lines of "as usual she and I do not agree on this matter". Such entries had appeared very rarely in the years prior to retirement. Had I changed, or had she? Or was it our new circumstances?

We had no master plan for our coming retirement years. Events and behaviour in our new "freedom" would evolve over time. We were not orphans, both our mothers were alive – one fiercely independent, the other reaching the point of being in care, both 200 miles away.

The first big decision was not the one common amongst retired people – that of downsizing – but one of upsizing so that we could accommodate our family comfortably when they visited.

Despite the temptation to move to a more central base to our family, we valued the life style in our current location so highly that we were in total agreement to stay in the area.

The mountain would have to come to Mohammed!

A significant decision was joining Probus. The fellowship, friendship and social activities added to our quality and enjoyment of life. We moved into our new home, without the stress that usually accompanies it.

Travel, new hobbies, our new home, kept us fully occupied. We discovered that one's income in retirement allowed us at least the quality of life enjoyed previously, but with the ingredients very much changed. We were really well off – and we do not mean financially, we mean spiritually.

The overall conclusion, drawing on our experience and the experiences of others of our age group, is that with proper planning one's income in retirement allows at least the quality of life enjoyed previously. In our case we have not felt financial constraints with regards to anything we wish to do and we know this relates to the planning process we engaged in early in our retirement, and plain good sense.

Where do we go from here?

'The most important things happen when we are unconscious.'

Can we beat the averages?

We are now in our mid-sixties (a generous description). We will take a look ahead at what might be our last ten years (if the averages don't change).

As we write the world is in financial chaos and the UK is officially in recession. We have not cared to look at its effect on our remaining investments, nor considered the possible effects on our pension. Most importantly our families do not seem pessimistic about the future, and that is good enough for us.

First though, let's reflect on that which has passed in the last 12 years. What have we learned about the strain on relationships that undoubtedly occurs when the main provider first retires from full time employment? We mean tensions that in some instances develop and grow as time passes and others that disappear!

Let us first be sexist and assume that provider is a man. He will, if in a profession, have been working in a dominantly democratic environment. Whatever his status he will have been used to a process whereby decisions are eventually made and which are then largely accepted and worked to. The wife, on the other hand, has been totally in charge of her environment – the home, her hobbies and interests and will not have consulted her partner about the day to day decisions she makes. Most important issues in the marriage will have been discussed and decisions made (if not in total agreement), but not the day to day issues.

So the man ceases work and continues to believe the environment in which he has worked for the last 30-40 years will exist at home. It does not, and it causes tensions. "If I am going to be expected to use a vacuum cleaner, surely I should have an input into the new model we are about to buy?" No!

"If I am going to cook us a meal today, surely I am in charge of the kitchen?" No!

The democratic process does not apply. So you change from the "shall we think about . . ." to "tomorrow we are going to . . ." This results in a totally predictable response (given your knowledge of your partner).

The other thing that is common amongst the female of the species is a huge desire to always be right. Man can debate an issue with one, two or twenty people and can often be heard to say, "Oh yes, I now understand your point of view and I clearly need to take another look at the issue". Not so the female of the species, especially in her own home. She is right, and that is it.

You may well have run a large company, a large department, engaged in life-changing research, advised thousands, but in your own home you are simply never right. In retirement your ability to think rationally and make decisions has apparently disappeared totally and the wide experience of many years left behind with your former employer.

No employee behaved in this way within the business environment. They would not have survived. But you, of course, did not love them, nor did you go to bed with them, looking, to you, as attractive and alluring as the day you first did so. (If you did go to bed with your employee – then you were being a very, very naughty boy or girl!).

Money causes tensions. When you worked you were used to the best. When an item was required for "the office" then it would be acquired and would be the top of its range. Snack lunches were of the highest quality and business lunches totally indulgent.

One's clothing had to be the smartest, price no object. You travelled first class, by rail or air, drove a top of the range car (or were driven).

This thinking inevitably transfers to retirement and your own home, but the system is now controlled by "she who must be obeyed".

Food is one area. Beef from Tesco is significantly cheaper than your local source. This is not only because of the economies of scale, but because they buy a beast yesterday and it is the joint you buy today. Conversion of cash spent into revenue lords it over quality considerations. So the slaughtered beast does not "hang" when butchered, as is the case with your local bloke (who is fast dying out thanks to Tesco and a largely indiscriminate new generation).

Was that a rant? Yes! Why don't people think further than their bank accounts?

Where was I? Oh yes, talking about money causing tensions. There is no doubt that the desire to save money leads to an acceptance of lower quality in food, drink and consumer goods, but must be fought.

If you do not do so you will sit down to prawn cocktail from a plastic tub, followed by tough, chewy, flavourless beef and rubbery cheese to finish with, all washed down by a £3 bottle of wine that you don't enjoy and followed by a cup of own label instant coffee from somewhere called Fair Trade. Your wife's hard work and skills will all have been in vain in order to create a "saving".

I could go on and on; the easy chair that saved you hundreds of pounds but is so uncomfortable that you don't sit in it; the jacket you didn't like but was a terrific bargain and now sits permanently at the back of the cupboard. Do I make my point? Don't save money at the expense of your quality of life. What will happen to what you save?

So into "the last ten years" you will have reached a compromise across all theatres of war and know that life can go on together and be totally enjoyable. You will have evolved a system in retirement whereby you pursue both your individual interests and the interests that have always been shared, or newly developed interests. We have developed these so our lives are full up to the point where we sometimes feel under pressure.

Those interests are cerebral, physical and artistic. What does the man of the house do? He shoots. He walks his dog every morning for 1-2 hours. He gardens (including half an acre of lawns that he mows manually). He plays crown green bowls, socially and competitively and, in the winter, indoor flat green bowls. He walks in the countryside.

He reads, writes, sets quizzes, watches television, paints, travels, enjoys drinking wine and single malt whiskies, belongs to Probus, studies military history and belongs to associated organisations and is a stamp collector. He has passed the advanced motoring test driving vacuum cleaners. He is totally committed to the family concept and supports them in any way that is acceptable and likes making preserves and cooking.

What does the lady of the house do? She plays short tennis and badminton, gardens, walks occasionally, plays bowls (outdoors and indoors, organises the running of the household (does most of it herself), watches television,

belongs to an active local ladies' group. She provides excellent food but seemingly without the pleasure some housewives get from this, does her bit in the garden and is the true expert (remembers all the names and how they should be cared for). Within the home she shows an admirable level of confidence in herself, which is not always so evident outside of the home.

She has adapted totally to the icons of modern living. Her mobile 'phone keeps her closely in touch with the family and is invaluable with the grandchildren and she is a wizard on the computer having mastered virtually all of the complex services it provides.

Himself, on the other hand, has rejected any involvement in modern technology. Mobile 'phones are an unacceptable intrusion into the privacy of his life and texts in particular he feels shield people from the reality of life and its relationships. Individuals will say things in texts that they would not voice face to face and divisions can occur much more frequently as a result. His stance on not having a mobile 'phone is based on these fears and others. He, of course, recognises their basic values but believes their wider use has and will change society in unacceptable ways.

He does not use computers in the sense that he will not sit in front of one and "be a button pusher". In his business life he was associated with a business group steeped in traditions of being at the forefront of development of computer science and usage and embraced those traditions but he would only use computers as a source of immediate information. Right to the end of his career he believed that verbal exchange of ideas in emotionally charged environments led to the creation of new ideas and proper resolution of problems and to ensuring their implementation took place on a shared basis.

So, in retirement, his wife not only enjoys her computer skills and their development, she provides a constant service to her husband and his many interests. He will never "push buttons!"

We will no doubt constantly review (on an informal basis) all our interests and hobbies, and accept some will decline over time, others burgeon and, who knows, new ones may be found.

We have observed through the experiences of others that there will be growing physical and mental constraints on our current pursuits. What will be important is to first fight those constraints, to eventually recognise their impact and to adapt to ensure our time is full. Vegetation will not be acceptable.

We love foreign travel, but getting there and back has become a dreadful experience that we tolerate for the bit in between. Friends figure large in our travels. We either visit them or go with them and travel infrequently on our own for shorter breaks, mostly when warmth is required. Our longer 'adventures' have culture, hobbies or sport (or a mix of these) at their core.

With grandchildren now reaching the point of owning cars, having part time jobs, entering university, entering first relationships, we suspect (but don't know) that we will see less of them. That will cause no unhappiness or friction on our parts as long as contact in some form is maintained (easy on the texts and e-mails!)

It is, of course, now increasingly possible that we might see more of their parents. They have established their life styles whilst their children have been growing up but spending more time with them would be good, especially whilst we are still active i.e. not perceived as 'old'.

An important part of longevity and good health is life style. All our interests ensure we exercise regularly and well. Necessity governs what we eat. My wife suffers from hypertension and high cholesterol levels. This requires medication as well as strong control of diet. I was diagnosed with late on-set diabetes, treated by diet and medication (under control) and my asthma requires inhalers. Neither of us allows these conditions to unduly influence lifestyle, other than diet.

Dietary needs are poles apart. He must have bread and potatoes for slow sugar release (and no sugar of course) and to control weight eat virtually nil fats, using unsaturated whenever they are needed. He must eat at regular intervals, little but often and eats huge amounts of fruit (those not containing sugar). He avoids wines with alcohol levels below 13% loves "sugar free" single malt whisky and drinks cider instead of beer (cider has around 2% sugar only).

She avoids potatoes and bread, eats vegetables instead. Also avoids saturated fats. Likes yoghurt and bananas particularly, but also enjoys eating fruit and drinks very little alcohol. She manages meals unselfishly leaning always towards his needs and then constructing her own meals around it.

We eat out fairly frequently. At lunch times usually snacks (he does not like "lunches"; strongly prefers "dinners") and in the evenings we can eat out on a functional "must have" basis or take longer with a leisurely but special atmosphere. It may not be a special celebration, but we make it so.

Eating out takes away the possibility of routine and drudgery that can arise around the need for food. Food and drink is a very important part of our life and we treat it as such. It is and will be the foundation of beating the averages.

With regards to illness and infirmities associated with getting older, we are determined to avoid that to which many seem to succumb. We refer to the desire to talk about them and to share infirmities with anyone who will lend a sympathetic ear.

In saying that, we do not refer to those experiencing a very real medical crisis in their lives and who need strong support of friends and family. Our comments relate to those who use them as a basis of conversation. Minor ailments should be brushed aside and conversation should be about intellectually demanding subjects that keep the brain on the move.

Sex is not an intellectually demanding subject, but through our lives has taken what we believe to be its proper place. We have never shared our perceptions of sex with other friends or family. It has not been necessary.

The pattern of our sex life has changed through indefinable phases of our life, but has only occasionally caused stress, which discussion between us has resolved. We know the longer term effects of diabetes can have negative effects but we also know those can be overcome by modern medications so we'll take that in our stride. Sex has always been fun and we see no reason why this should not continue to be the case. We'll find out in due course.

That provides a link to conflict. The constant thread through our 50 years plus of association has been our love for each other. This has never meant that we have not been prepared for frank, and sometimes stormy, exchanges of views. Resolution of differences, if not always as a result of democratic process, has always taken place. I cannot see that changing and would not want such a change. Differences are inevitable and they emerge from changing lifestyle, changing circumstances. They should be resolved, not allowed to simmer below the surface.

Now to the role of money/finance in beating the averages: money has never worried me in any way. It was not a subject that particularly interested me when young and it does not now. I can always remember changing my bank (on their request) and moving from a Manager called Fudge to a different company's bank, where the Manager was Mr Honey. The latter also threw me out. Two real sweeties!

A bank, and more importantly a younger manager, took me on understanding the confidence I had in myself and I stayed with them for the next 30 years even when I moved home; I am sure I justified their confidence.

My wife, who had to manage a home and children through the leanest of years, is understandably more cautious about money. She saves me money all the time and I devise ingenious ways of spending it. To my knowledge, once into solvency, I have never denied (nor ever would deny) her anything she wanted.

We have no detailed financial plan for the future. We will support our family in any way they might need. I'll run my car until it breathes its final breath and then we'll settle for one vehicle. We value the independence of being a two car family currently, despite the prohibitive cost. We'll let the car decide.

The averages indicate that I, the man of the house, will pop my clogs first. The good old-fashioned, wonderful company pension fund will continue to pay my wife around two thirds of the current total and maintain other benefits such as private medical care, so we have no worries there. (She says not having to buy wine and whisky will equate to the lost third!)

Our forward thinking says that, by the time of that event, we will have been settled in a new smaller home chosen for the latter part of our lives. Will it be near our present home? Near the family? Near other friends? Who knows, and we don't have to decide until nearer the time.

When we do "downsize" (what an awful term) I'll buy myself a top of the range Mercedes convertible with the capital released and when I then pop my clogs she says she'll hire a "nice young man" to drive it for her. It's good to have plans and ambitions.

Whatever old age holds, when it comes we will deal with it as we have the successive ages within our lives – childhood, the school years, marriage, raising a family, developing our careers and retirement – by enjoying it.

The rowan tree

When as a child, I could not see
The sadness in the Rowan tree.
For I was then too young to know
The silent hatred of the doe.
But I have learnt the words of love,
The bitter venom of the dove.
Where is that child, sad Rowan tree ?
Are your bright berries tears for me ?

The sailor's wife

How brave is my sailor with friends and good cheer,
With his stories of oceans so wild.
But he cries in his dreams
In my arms through the night
In his fear, in his fear, in his fear.

How jaunty his cap with his buttons and braid,
And his journeys around the world wide.
But I hold him so close
In my arms through the night
To be near, to be near, to be near.

Now his grave is unknown in the cold cruel sea,
With his stories and name all forgot.
But he comes to me still
In my arms through the night
Ever dear, ever dear, ever dear.

Window of privilege

During my boyhood, I cannot remember any discussion of retirement in my family. I did notice that in my father's and my grandfathers' generation not all of them had had the well ordered and comfortable home of my charming Uncle Harold. Harold was ok. He had a thing called a 'pension'. The others did not. Most of them continued working as long as they could and maybe drew a miniscule pension. The fact that a pension was 'a good thing' was tucked away at the back of my mind.

Having graduated, I was qualified to take up house surgeon posts. Here willy nilly I became a member of the National Health Service Superannuation scheme (NHS).

The exemption from National Service runs out and we were destined for call up. The NHS authorities wrote to say that our accumulated superannuation money could be reclaimed if we wished. If we left it with them they would very generously continue to pay their contribution, i.e. two years' contributions – a 'no brainer' as far as I was concerned – offer accepted.

While in various posts in Manchester we had good liaison with, and worked in, other hospital oral surgery units. Now Gerry Mellor headed the one at Crumpsall, North Manchester. One day he told us that he had enquired of the Regional Hospital Board for how long a Consultant drew his pension on retiring at age 65 years? The answer was" 18 months on average", eighteen months only! However, retirement aged 62 years on grounds of ill health gave survival for a further 10 years on average.

Years later, now in Sheffield, I remembered the shock, horror on Gerry Mellor's face when he learnt this. Discreetly via friends and acquaintances I made the same enquiry of our Area Health Authority. The average was round about the same, 18 months to two years. The point was noted.

Reaching my 63rd birthday, the University finance department told me that, as I had been superannuated for 40 years, no more contributions were required from them, or me. Much as I enjoyed my job there was a lot to think about, including the history I have just outlined.

When Sir Paul Bramley retired in 1988 I took over as temporary head of department with all that that entailed, until the new professor was appointed and I could hand things back to him. Peter Robinson eventually arrived. He is a true academic, interested in clinical work to a degree but his greatest love is research, a big plus factor as far as the University was concerned. Having got his feet under the table, surveyed his empire, he asked me to take on the Department again so once more I became its Head. Fortunately we had already a superb team. Though I say it myself teaching was well organized, service to the patients excellent with very good liaison with the NHS consultants and their staff. I was helped by marvellous administrative and secretarial men and women.

After much thought I decided to go early. So I gave a year's notice of my intention, to finish in October 1994. This gave a long notice time enabling what I hope was a smooth hand over for all the responsibilities. They were numerous. Both University and NHS colleagues were most helpful in achieving this.

So what were the downsides you may ask?

Once you announce the intention to retire you find out rapidly that you become sidelined. You are no longer included in committees, meetings etc., which are discussing and arranging events due to happen after you have gone. Quite right too, but it is sad for you. Then when you have departed there is the inevitable break in routine, which can be unsettling. There is no more early rising for ward rounds at 8am. No tutorials after clinics, no staying on to dictate the clinic notes, no cut and thrust of the committees. Of course it was nice to have the free time, the burden of responsibility lifted—but one missed the companionship of colleagues, and the joy of seeing students mature and graduating. The loss of the clinical challenge of patients, their diagnoses and treatment, was counterbalanced by the freedom from emergency call out!

It was such a delight to have more time at home, with Tricia who had been most supportive all these years. Delight, too, for more time with the family and for community activities. One of the inevitable questions one gets asked when you say you are retiring is 'What are you going to do?' said rather pityingly as though that was the end of the world. I have known colleagues panic at the thought, struggling to maintain contact with 'work' in some form or other as though otherwise their world would collapse. How sad for them.

For me a whole host of activities beckoned almost too numerous to mention. Here are some: The family, garden, home, bowls, swimming, school governor, computing skills to be learnt, family history exploration, TA activities, Church warden. These prove more than enough to occupy all the time available, besides many courses offered by local colleges.

One hobby I must give you in more detail and that's fishing.

Ken Moore, an esteemed colleague at the Northern General Hospital, asked me the usual question and rather as a throwaway line at the end of the list I said, 'Well maybe I would do a spot of fishing'. I did not know he was a very keen fisherman. He quizzed me and I had to confess my experience in that direction was mainly with a bent pin and a trip to a canal with my grandfather. He remonstrated that I should be taught and taught properly too.

A few days later bless him, he sent through the post details of where he was taught. The Arundel Arms, no less, at Lifton in Devon, a beautiful, cosy country pub, which is famous for sporting courses, shooting as well as fishing. I sent for the brochures. We could not go that year 1994, but the next May saw Tricia and I off on a five-day visit. Tricia busied herself with the local scenery with other wives and partners and chatting up the Chef who was part of the set up. Anne Vos Barke (Husband Conrad Vos Barke—a famous journalist) owns the place. The two ghillies took the twelve of us on the course under their wing. A fabulous time with excellent tuition ranging from the environment, feeding habits of fish, insect life, equipment, how to cast, choice of flies – and we caught fish too! At the end we were all full of enthusiasm coming back home determined to seek out fishing here, which of course I did. First on the River Noe, then via a waiting list to the Derwent Fly Fishing Club, which has been magic.

There is an old saying between husband and wife along the lines 'I married you for better or for worse, but not for lunch'. How true. A man retiring, now at home all day, is inevitably invading his wife's space so it is so important to have sufficient space in the house, each to have their own space, to have their own activities separately as well as those they enjoy together. In my case this, though true, was somewhat reversed. Tricia was part time Matron at Birkdale Boys' School and did not retire until 1997, so I had the house to myself for a year or two establishing my routine. The house, time, space, were largely all mine for most of the day, so I well appreciate the adjustments that have to be made when both are retired. It just takes a modicum of common sense and flexibility to adjust and compromise.

Most important is to keep fit, active and enjoy family holidays you can have together, hobbies that are separate and/or combined. I must say that preparation for all this was helped also by the offer of a 'Retirement course' run by the NHS authorities where they gave us information on a whole host of problems we might face, new situations we would encounter and ideas about retirement. It ranged from legal matters, wills, finance, pensions and where to get help if needed. It included medical problems as one aged, how to acquire new skills – even gardening and cooking. It was a most useful and enterprising bonus for staff.

So, retirement is nothing to be feared, merely another stage upon our journey. It is to be grasped eagerly, to be enjoyed to the full. Mind you, one finds that 'time' appears to accelerate, so go to it, enjoy your friends and of course Probus!

Like others of my contemporaries, I have been privileged to belong to a final salary scheme. It still seems to be solvent! A steady job for life and solid recompense after work underpins the sort of retirement I have described. It is not the likely pattern for the young, neither was it the pattern of most of my predecessors. So I am very fortunate to be enjoying this window of good fortune.

Unreal expectations?

When one is young, the word "retirement" conjures up a vision of a future existence in which everything wonderful is possible and one is completely relieved of the cares of working life with all its responsibilities and frustrations. Nothing can be further from the truth in many cases but in others the reality can be nearer to the utopia wished for.

I very much looked forward to my retirement, not because my working environment was no longer attractive - in fact this was far from the case. It was because I had a vision of a different type of existence in which I was not constrained by timetables and continual responsibilities not of my making. In fact, I would be able to do anything I wanted at any time and thus enter a new exciting life in the years to come.

I was given the opportunity to retire earlier than I had expected, but three years before this was to take place my future plans were given a sudden jolt. My wife and I were to spend Christmas with our family but I had developed a severe chest infection and although feeling unwell managed to make the journey. After returning home, my wife noticed that I had developed a rash of purple spots and that this was present all over my body. I assumed that this was caused by the infection or some spicy Christmas food but my wife made me see my GP. Leukaemia was suspected but bone marrow and blood tests showed that I had developed the rare blood condition called idiopathic autoimmune thrombocytopenic purpura. Treatment was by prolonged dosage with steroids and a possible spleen removal to try to stimulate the production of blood platelets. Otherwise I would be faced with a life marred by continual spontaneous bruising and bleeding problems.

My vision for our future retirement was now clouded by the possible effects of this blood condition. I would have to be very careful of any activity which might cause bruising or bleeding. This complaint did not in itself affect my general health but the steroids made me very unwell with little increase in platelet production. My wife persuaded me to discuss with the consultant the possibility of stopping the steroids. I decided not to risk a spleen removal, as there was no guarantee that this would solve the problem. I now take no medication, I have very little bruising and few bleeding problems and I am quite fit and healthy. I retired after a few years and have lived with this complaint ever since (over twenty years).

The moral of this story is that most people look forward to retirement with the anticipation of wonderful times ahead for many years, but the reality may be very different. With advancing age, one can expect deterioration in health and possible disablement leading to a curtailment in the expected wonderful leisure time spreading into the future. I have been fortunate in that my complaint, which could have been life threatening, although sometimes a nuisance, has not affected my general health and well being. My wife, although she has had several surgical operations to improve her mobility, is reasonably healthy. Even so, we have not been able to take full advantage of the freedom of our retirement years. For many people, plans for an active retirement may not materialise as expected especially if cognitive functions become impaired as well as general health deterioration. However, a positive adjustment to the change in circumstances is essential if happiness is to be assured. A healthy life-style, involving plenty of gentle exercise, a balanced diet, and mental activity helps the adjustment. Involvement with the affairs of children and grandchildren, an active social life with friends and taking up new interests and hobbies all add colour and stimulus.

All being well, retirement is a wonderful part of our life cycle provided that we make the best of it under circumstances beyond our control.

A parrot called Cassius

'The fascination of what's difficult
Has drained the sap of my veins, and rent
Spontaneous joy and natural content
Out of my heart.'

This is W.B. Yeats in sombre mood. I read this the other day and it struck home with some truth.

My life as an academic had indeed schooled me into an analytical and critical approach to ideas and projects. This is essential to the furtherance of knowledge. The scrutiny of potential publications of others and one's self, for instance, as well as "The fascination with what's difficult" demanded a cold, critical, pernickety and substantially objective attitude. The climate in a science based subject leaves room for little else.

In retirement, I now realize that this working experience has left me with a lopsided outlook. It is not over dramatic to say it has 'Rent spontaneous joy and natural content out of my heart.' However, it is wrong to put all the blame on my job. There must have been seeds in my own personality, which have flourished in this environment.

Nevertheless retirement requires a substantial change. A critical, objective attitude to people and events really won't do. There is an emotional hole. It is not easy to relax, to enjoy, be generous, be accepting, be content or even to be 'touchy-feely'.

What can be done? Well, I have made a start. I have recognized the general difficulty. When these old and unhelpful traits show themselves again and again, I recognize and smile at them and give them the brush off.

Consciously then, I must try to make room for acceptance and generosity and smile a lot more.

Maybe a gradual and progressive change will improve the balance between brain and heart?

'He thinks too much. Such men are dangerous.'
William Shakespeare, *Julius Caesar*, Act1 Scene 2

What about depression? – Churchill's 'Black Dog'

If it strikes, is it connected with retirement?

Is the fundamental change from a structured work pattern to a free-range life a contributory factor?

Has it been there for years, but held at bay? If it is there, how does one tackle it?

Getting deeply involved and committed to an activity may help – writing a book, working with a charity, learning to play a musical instrument are possibilities. Any of these could help with short-term onset of depression but it is doubtful whether they would do anything for a deep-seated condition.

Attitudes in the working community to anyone with mental health problems have been pretty terrible over the years. Attitudes and opinions tended to stick like leeches and so the natural reaction (and possibly necessary safeguard) was to hide anything which could possibly suggest "he/she is not quite up to the job".

In retirement, all of that can be left behind. And it is possible to say, "I have a life to live and I want to live it to the full. I want to look at the things which damage my health and well-being, to understand them and so to be able to challenge them".

The question arises – "How?"

Whatever answer one comes up with takes courage – the courage to say, "I want help".

Counselling is a possibility but it can be a bit like sticking a plaster on a running sore, stopping the blood flow but not dealing with the cause.

Psychoanalysis is another approach. This can be painful, take a long time (maybe years) and it costs money. With a good analyst, things which have seriously impacted on one's life but have lain hidden, can be brought into recognition, looked at, considered and acknowledged as a part of the whole person.

Accepting help may be daunting; is one admitting that one is less than perfect, less than capable of dealing with any situation, less than totally strong?

Maybe so.

But back to the earlier comments, life is for living to the full. Tackling and dealing with anything which restricts that is surely valuable.

As a child, I went into the study of my grandfather, Winston Churchill. "Grandpa," I said, "Is it true that you are the greatest man in the world?" "Yes, now b***** off." – *Nicholas Soames*

Getting old

Getting old, who's getting old?
Of course it isn't me
I'm just as strong as ever
Except perhaps my knee.

I have to wear my spectacles
To drive and watch TV
The hearing aid fits nicely
Getting old? No not me.

Perhaps I can't run quite so fast
But then I never could
High heels seem to hurt my feet
My legs don't look quite so good
I've put a bit of weight on
But I'm eating the right food
Perhaps there are more calories now
Or maybe it's my blood.

Drink more water is the message
From the government today
And so I do, but need the loo
More and more each day!
A little snooze right after lunch
Is good for you they say
So this I do, just close my eyes
It gives me chance to pray.

Getting old can be quite fun
If with friends you have a laugh
You have a meal, a little drink
Remember things quite daft.
Things don't worry you so much
Saying something wrong or making a gaff
Everybody does it
So why not just laugh.

Start with pudding

Life is uncertain, start with pudding.

A very glib statement but it could have much deeper significance.

Through one's early years and then as an ingrained attitude, one had to work hard for the good things.

The old Yorkshire saying "One who eats most pudding can have most meat" was a variant, filling up with stodge before getting a chance to have the best bit, the meat. An economic approach in hard times.

Partnership on a pension

Ah fill the cup – what boots it to repeat
How time is slipping underneath our feet;
Unborn tomorrow and dead yesterday,
Why fret about them if today be sweet.

Edward Fitzgerald

Retirement may be obligatory at a certain age as in government service, age and rank related as in the services, or voluntary in self-employment; an eighty year old may prefer to remain in charge of his business! However, apart from those who are determined to die at the helm or those made redundant, retirement is often a predictable event, which allows time for preparation and planning. As a health service doctor I knew that 65 was the age at which I would have to retire from the National Health Service (NHS).

In marriage and partnership there is likely to be a steady progress from conjugation to parenthood to an "empty nest". These events are best managed if both partners can discuss and plan for change. If this has been the norm, retirement can be approached in the same way; retirement ideally is a shared process. Sometimes retirement is a separate event for each partner, the need for shared plans remains the same. On the contrary a single person is used to making unilateral decisions or to discussing change with others, both are important. Whilst the impact on a partner is not an issue, planning and consultation remain essential.

Beti was concerned that I would miss the balance between work and home to which I was used. We identified our main shared interests outside the family as walking, gardening and playing bridge and made definite plans to expand and improve these activities. With her encouragement, I put my name down on the waiting lists for Hope Valley Probus and Cavendish Decorative and Fine Arts Society. Her input into my retirement plans was significant!

Retirement may not be a once in a lifetime experience; some friends had careers in the services, retired in their early 50s and found a new career. As a radiologist I was involved both in patient care and in the management of a department with a budget for staffing, equipment and expendables. A move into a non-clinical post was therefore possible without a complete change of lifestyle. I decided to take Bar Exams and attempt to become a Coroner, however the regulations changed and required a full time studentship up to the part 1B examination Such a move came later when I became chief of a new NHS Trust for my last three working years. Retiring from a different job was, in my experience, an easier move. The hospital survived and prospered and I retired with a sense of achievement whereas to retire after thirty years in the same speciality would have been much more difficult.

The ambition of a twenty or thirty year old drives many people along their career path, by the age of fifty realism should enable some ambitions to be discarded. This is an important process otherwise unfulfilled targets will spill over into retirement as a cause of bitterness. As a member of Council in two professional bodies I looked at the possibility of becoming President, neither opportunity arose but recognition in my own sub-speciality gave me an ample return.

If one is prepared to take on tasks outside one's everyday work it is more likely that such opportunities will continue after retirement. Experience of and involvement in voluntary organisations is rewarding and likely to continue after retirement. The Territorial Army, The Order of St John, The Railton Owners Club, The British Legion and arts societies keep me active after retirement, acting as chairman in some instances. The first four did not involve Beti but were accepted and gave us some time to pursue different interests.

Retirement is a step in the "seven ages" and inevitably illness, physical or mental, will form a part of the ageing process. Coping with these challenges should be helped if a plan for retirement has succeeded and the principle of partnership planning established.

Presently, we are both fit enough to pursue our various interests and aim to keep fit; experience tells us however that the future is unpredictable.

Those of us with grown-up children look forward to being grandparents, offering support and encouragement but avoiding unwanted advice and interference. However the expectations of an "Indian summer" may be upset for various reasons such as loss of contact, under-achievement, or serious illness in grandchildren.

Beti and I have ten grandchildren, three of whom have various degrees of paralysis and are wheel chair bound. We offer support in day-to-day activities, and financially, towards the building of a suitable house and arranging holidays. Difficulties arise as the grandchildren become bigger and we are less able physically to lift them, a new male partner is difficult to "get on" with and we are concerned about our daughter's health with continuous mental and physical strain. I attempt to take a pragmatic view that we can only do what is asked of us within physical and financial limits. Beti is more involved and frustrated by our inabilities and disagreements with the new partner. Previously she would spend at least two days a week with the family, now we more often meet them away from their home. This situation will continue to cause anxiety and we have to try to identify those matters where we can offer help and those outside our ability to intervene.

Finally, a shared faith can provide a firm foundation for the journey through the years of retirement. This may be based on religious belief, charitable activities, politics and other deeply held convictions. We are both Anglicans but find that the journey away from "1662" causes problems which outbalance the perceived need to modernise. However we have the same views to share. Christianity is not an hour on Sunday but going to church should reinforce faith and not produce a feeling that change may alienate the elderly without attracting the young, some of whom respond to tradition and ceremony.

That's the way it is folks

A few years ago I received a setback in my war against an invasion of grey squirrels.

I lined up the crosswires on the telescopic sight of the air rifle and squeezed the trigger. I caught the recoil round my right eye. The squirrel hopped away unharmed.

Looking in the mirror through that eye, I could not see anything of that eye except a bluish blur. Was it a detached retina?

To cut a long story short, it turned out to be age related macular degeneration, and must have been developing long before the rifle incident. Macular degeneration of the dry type is common in the over sixties and is the most frequent cause of sight loss in the developed countries. It causes a progressive deterioration of eyesight leaving very peripheral vision only.

There is little or nothing that can be done about it in a preventive or therapeutic sense. How did I deal with the news? Not very well really. In accepting the diagnosis, I realised something of what it might mean. From time to time it causes irritation and immense frustration particularly in reading and computer usage. Both can be done but very slowly and often inaccurately. One has to admit that it improves the vocabulary of the vernacular.

Of course there are aids available ranging from a decent light and magnifying glass to sophisticated electronic devices.

I know I compare badly with the heroic example of a friend in our village. An academic in his nineties, he is struggling to complete a major book of considerable importance. He has persisted with reading, writing, researching and proof reading for many, many months using what's left of his eyesight for 12 hours a day. He has reached a crippling stage of macular degeneration when most sufferers would have thrown in the towel years ago. Yes, he's made it; publication date is announced!

The message is - accept the disability, get on with it and stop complaining.

Losing sight is a particular example of what has been described as "The death of a thousand cuts."

The cuts occur throughout life and may be of greater or lesser importance. During retirement and associated ageing, the cuts come faster and can be more upsetting. Failure in all its variety, divorce, loss of friends, family or partner, a menacing medical diagnosis and retirement itself, the cuts are a thousand fold by definition. One of these is the realisation that you really are old. We acknowledge the reduction of stamina, energy, physical strength, mobility, increasing deafness, chronic pain, memory loss, sudden nominal aphasia and much else. But there is a time and it's a sobering one when you realise others see you as you are – a dithering old man to be pitied. You are almost treated as a non-person. You know the stance, "Does he take sugar?"

The thousand cuts are part of life in general and represent in their acute forms a major part of the challenge of old age.

There must be many ways of coping with the challenge. Sometimes there is a strong temptation to give up, admit defeat and go into miserable depression. Others are able to recognize each cut as it comes, face the implications, see what help is available and look for positive ways of ameliorating the effects. They accept their situation with a shrug of the shoulders saying "That's the way it is folks". They are able to rejoice in the continuation of life and enjoy the things they still can do. They don't pine for the past.

Listen to Margaret's story, it puts these matters into perspective.

She was a happy, outgoing woman and a considerable tennis player. Her family life was good, raising four children.

Her husband on retirement became depressed. She did not know the cause but it became clear that her husband was a practising bisexual. How long this state of affairs had been going on she never knew. They separated.

About this time, she found she had breast cancer, which was treated by surgery and radiotherapy. There were recurrent secondaries with several episodes of fractures and spine and skull involvement.

Assorted chemotherapy with all its side effects was used on each occasion. Not only did she survive 20 years but lived these years in a remarkably positive and happy way. She was sustained by the support of her children and her practical Christian faith.

Strangers

Now all the world and gentle time
Become the strangers of my mind.
The world began when I was old,
My journeys done, my stories told.
The world will end when I am young,
My heart unused, my love unsung.
This wasted world for all of time,
The last companion of my mind.

The Winter Rose

Old men remember spring,
Forget the wealth of summer.
When now and then are one
Each day is like another.
In youth there was no rest
Without the mountain air.
In age it is enough
To get up from my chair.
The friends I have will fade,
Each melting with my past.
My prayers are not for them
But that I am not last.
Old men remember spring,
Forget the wealth of summer.
The winter rose is cruel
With promise of hereafter.

A change of tempo

Breakfast on the hoof or not at all, was the norm. Now it's delightfully different. No children, no grand children about, just a quiet simple breakfast for two with delectable fresh black coffee. Then a few minutes of reading aloud, sometimes it is 'Poem for the Day' from Wendy Cope's collection, a Jane Austen novel or an 'improving' book.

It often turns out to be a special time during the day – unhurried, contemplative, the pleasures of the moment. Sometimes, even, significant communication happens!

Be nice to your kids – they'll be choosing your Nursing Home!

Age is a very high price to pay for maturity.

Community spirit

It is well known that the age of the population is increasing due to the advances made in medical science. As a consequence of this, one would hope that, in an ideal world, community spirit in the elderly would keep pace with the needs of people in the community, especially those whose lives have been devastated by the loss of a lifelong partner. Unfortunately, that does not seem to be the case for reasons I outline below. In the beginning of adult life the forward looking interests of both sexes create a togetherness in which both sides actively seek the company and interest of each other and this process is ongoing until the right partner for life's journey is found. Even if early judgments prove to be unsound, the game does not stop there and the search for a lasting partner continues. This urgent seeking of the right partner or company does not seem to be mirrored in later years and it seems to me that once the early ambitions of togetherness and family have been realised there is little interest in looking for friendship or company between the sexes.

There would be no need for this note if the consequences of increasing age were broadly equal among the sexes, but the astonishing fact is that the male population in the UK have shorter lives than their female counterparts by a significant margin. This national statistic is well known and at one time amounted to a gap of 7 years, approaching approximately a 10% difference in lifespan. Of course there are many instances which would seem to contradict this fact, but the statistic is unquestionable.

I have often wondered how this difference in longevity came about. The answers to this question must be complex. One jokey answer is that men work harder than women in their respective lifetimes, but I am confident that this is not the case. Anyone fortunate enough to have been close to the raising of children and the support of family needs in the home will know of the multi-tasking abilities of women which call for huge inputs of energy and enthusiasm which I do not think are matched by men in the workplace. For men, the paramount issue is to seek and find employment, which is suited to their abilities and to become so proficient that their employment is secure. In the course of time the ever increasing demands in the family make it imperative that they compete for higher office and the benefits success brings. Thus reliability and depth of individual skills are more important for men and multi-tasking is not an issue.

If the jokey answer is not the case, then what is? Could it be that men are biologically designed in their genes to be doomed to a shorter lifespan? This must be a possibility.

I think it more likely that age and the lifetime practice of skills and responsibilities engender psychological differences. To expand on this, women's daily life goes on unchanged when retirement years begin, but a man faces the precipice of being important in the workplace one day and having no function to drive his days the next. Of course, a well planned retirement can help with this. To follow chosen hobbies more vigorously such as golf, the playing of the game of bridge, or fishing are examples of such hobbies, which might help. In the long run this is not the answer as the results of age will inevitably affect performance and thus the joy and fulfilment of such hobbies will decline. If no other activity has been found to fill the gap, then a man is left with nothing. In short, women are better suited to enjoy retirement years whilst for men it is a constant struggle to maintain the structure or discipline of the years in the workplace.

The situation outlined above becomes more critical when one or the other of a partnership is separated, either by choice, through divorce or by death. Women can maintain their lives with lifetime friends, and continue to live in their homes without undue stress. In the other case, a man is suddenly faced with the responsibilities of running a home and looking after himself, whilst finding that his acceptability in a social environment is unfavourably changed. I think this leads to a sense of isolation with a tendency for withdrawal from social life, except perhaps from male dominated clubs such as the Probus.

In summary, a good community spirit is made by people who care for each other. As the Good Book says, "Love thy neighbour as thyself" and not as I heard one lady say recently in my company "I've had the best; you can keep the rest". If this is a common feeling amongst widows in the U.K., it's no wonder that men become lonely and find it difficult to make and enjoy a social life. That there are difficulties with individual openness is obviously not a secure way to solve this situation. Within the community there must be a more open, friendly way of including everybody with perhaps a bit less of "I've done my bit". I would hope that this openness, in the course of time, would improve social awareness for men and perhaps reduce the lifespan difference between men and women.

Stay away!

Stay away from the doctor. The only treatment for failing memory and stamina is a sense of humour.

Three things

Three things are essential for happiness: a loving wife, a warm bed and an empty bladder.

The first time

Years ago, on a crowded bus in Cambridge I was standing and a pretty girl sitting opposite smiled at me. I thought jolly good but then she offered me her seat. It was the first time that I realised I had grown old.

Yorlright then? Hooseyer sel?

Whether in South Yorkshire or Glasgow the question asks the same thing, "How are you?" However couched, this must be the commonest question asked in retirement.

I never know how to deal with it asking or replying.

Illness is a subject which has a fascination for the ageing. A few years ago, we hosted a lunch party for six of our retired colleagues. It began well enough until the question "How are you" was raised. Illness and disease then dominated the table; no amount of effort by us, as hosts, to change the agenda was successful. We felt cheated of what should have been a delightful and entertaining social occasion.

I fear when I ask the question that I might be standing on one foot or the other for an hour or so listening to someone else's obsession.

The motives for asking the question are varied; often it's an unthinking greeting, sometimes it's pure nosiness, a deluded kindness or a creepy seeking for approval.

It may be used as a visiting card for recounting medical horror stories, a competitive recital of woes and therapies often ending up with "Well I've had it worse than you." More rarely it signifies a concern for the other person. I now find it more comfortable and a lot safer to ask the question when it arises, without doubt, from a real concern.

Answering the question is much more trying. I just don't like to get into this area and resort to smart answers to turn away the question.

"Oh do you want the short answer or the truth."

"Well much the same only more so."

"Not on fortunes cap the very button."

"As well as can be expected for the time of the year."

"Getting on you know."

A bright smile and "I'm very happy."

"Fancy seeing you again I thought we were both dead."

"I must pinch myself to see if I am alive."

None of these smart replies does much to deepen friendship but they don't half stop the development of a competitive health exchange.

On further consideration it might be better to "get back to basics" as that nice Mr. Major used to say and pray the Nun's Prayer: "I ask for grace enough to listen to the tales of other's pains. But seal my lips on my own aches and pains – they are increasing, and my love of rehearsing them is becoming sweeter as the years go by. Help me to endure them with patience."

A woman's take on "How are you?"

I now find myself trying to prepare for a defence system should I make contact with those who may dare to ask – "How are you?"

The telephone is the worst of all enemies – there can be no backing off, save only that one listens and waits. Here it comes! A babble of words, indistinguishable in context, a complete history of medical conditions even verging on to a crisis of such proportions that the mind boggles when receiving this information. A sympathetic "Oh" – a sigh. "Really" is offered, only to be ignored whilst the wailing continues on and on until the realisation that the time is up and that all the details have dried up and can no longer be repeated. The telephone can now return to its normal function as a communication device.

Am I a happy bunny? Yes! I suppose I am. Perhaps the title of agony aunt is appropriate. What can I do to prepare myself for the next time? Next time will come again and again and again. Perhaps being a good listener is the secret, but one thing is for sure – it is a universal help-line and a comfort zone for those who sadly are confronted with their personal worries and welcome a sympathetic ear.

Sometimes, it is very refreshing when greeting someone by saying "How are you?" to receive a reply which is quite simply, "OK, I'm fine".

"What do you do with all your time?"

This is said to be the second most common question addressed by those still working to those who have retired. A pretty cheeky question really. We might be up to all sorts of no good. But then we probably aren't. I will try in a moment or two to answer precisely the question as drawn but before I do am making certain assumptions. First, that the enquirer is still working his socks off but is contemplating his own retirement. Second, that he has a wife who is also his best friend and that between them they have long since sorted out their respective domestic roles and have agreed on each other's need for space. (I say "he" because I am a he and I have been asked to speak from my own experience.) Third, that the enquirer is sufficiently healthy to pursue activities that interest him. Lastly, that major financial commitments have been dealt with (mortgage repayments, pension contributions etc.) so that money, whilst still subject to the discipline of a careful joint budget, is not a problem.

Right now - that question. What do I do with all that time? Don't read on if you are looking for exciting revelations. This is what I actually do in an average week and it isn't just random, it is based on a structured plan, which I made for myself before retirement. To make sure the body functions reasonably well, I take a fair amount of exercise. That includes tennis, walking my dogs every day and walking 10 miles or so with friends every week. That way, I get the feel good factor of exercise plus the company of good pals. (Remember that you are just about to lose the company of good colleagues at work.)

Then, to try and stem the onset of senility I put my brain under modest pressure by attending two weekly classes run by the WEA (Workers' Educational Association. The word workers is somewhat ironic when I look around at my colleagues in the class).

But three cheers for the WEA. I currently attend classes on the History of Art and the Development of the Concerto. Classes last just short of two hours and there is no compulsory homework. Then, I have to assuage my social conscience. I did this by having a lot of fun driving the community bus, but I have now been thrown out on the grounds of old age, and the roads are possibly the safer for it. I am also a footpaths inspector for a large tract of the White Peak. This suits my dogs, and I suspect I will not be thrown out of that job until I drop dead. What else? Lots of little things. I like to keep a clean desk and so spend a modest part of every day dealing with domestic paperwork. I sleep between 5 and 6pm to recharge the batteries. I take a lot of pills and have to remember to re-order them on time. I spend too long reading the daily paper and not nearly long enough reading books. I don't (can't) do crosswords and sudoku and don't watch much television but very much enjoy going to the cinema and theatre. Oh yes, and I seem to spend ages dressing and undressing to meet the demands of different activities. Very boring, and very different from the old days in the office.

Well there you have it. The question was asked and I have laid bare my soul. It doesn't have the makings of a novel but it makes for a fairly full life. Come to think of it, I have not dealt with treats, by which I mean holidays, travel and family. 14 years ago, when I retired, I immediately took two months out and sailed round the UK with my sons. That was a cracking start. Since then holidays, and the planning of them, have been an obsession. Having targets and making plans adds zest. But the basis of it is the structured weekly plan. I pursue activities, which keep me in touch with younger minds. I don't employ anyone. I sweep my own backyard. However, the foremost of my failures concerns that nagging social conscience. No mention of charitable work. I had my belly full of committees and chairmanships before I retired and determined to be hands on after retirement. No, I don't want a computer. I would rather be back on those buses.

People matter

Pre-retirement. My employer offered a pre-retirement course 12 months prior to my expected retirement date. The two main aspects were health and finance. The health aspect was somewhat depressing but no doubt realistic in that one has to face the problems of ageing but I was not prepared to accept deterioration. On the other hand it was a reminder to keep active mentally and physically for as long as possible.

The financial advice, given by someone completely independent of my employer's business, was very useful particularly for someone like me who was pretty ignorant about such matters. I used their advice and believe, with a few changes over the years, it has paid off.

Post-retirement. I dabbled at a number of brain-stimulating occupations such as learning German, improving my IT skills, which I now use mainly for photographic printing and archiving, basic piano lessons to help me to read music, which is useful for another hobby, singing choral music.

Physical fitness is easy so far and enjoyable. I've always loved walking and photography and what better countryside is there than the Peak District, my local area for those purposes? A small group, of similar age and ability, take it in turns to organise a route fortnightly. Usually we cover about 8 miles (10 miles when we started these walks 10 years ago).

Gardening is half chore and half enjoyment, but I know it's good exercise and I like to see the rewards of my efforts.

As a child I had four siblings and schooling years brought me into contact with a lot of people. My work also involved much person to person contact. I need people around me and I'm not happy on my own for very long.

When asked by an ex colleague some two years after I had retired, if I missed the buzz, the immediate answer was "no". Having given this question further thought, I realised the answer was somewhat hasty. I do miss the buzz created by the company of my colleagues during leisure time but pleased to be free from the pressure associated with my work. This is why I find my membership of Probus so stimulating and satisfying.

'Luck be a lady tonight'

It is said that you make your own luck but my luck started with my genes. I was born happy, into a loving family with a temperament that is not over demanding of others or myself. My losses and disappointments have been manageable, parents dying at a good age and two siblings still alive. I would have liked a large family but I have a wonderful daughter and two grandsons.

My husband died at the age of 66, early for these days, but he suffered from diabetes. One heart attack, followed by another eight weeks later, ensured that he was spared many possible horrors. He would have hated the complications of his illness.

The first thing I discovered about bereavement was that the books did not help much: the process is not one of progressive stages. Within six months I could find contentment for several hours – with some guilt. Yet it took me six years, and five of psychoanalysis, before I could write the following poem and understand my marriage enough to allow myself to be a whole person again.

I had started to write two weeks after my husband's death on the suggestion of my oldest friend. I have never been able to spell; my sister and mother were the writers in my family. I put a notebook by my bed and wrote whatever and whenever. I had done some medical editing and written a book on psychosexual medicine for doctors but I had nothing left to say to the profession. After taking several Open College of the Arts courses and obtaining an MA in creative writing, I tried short stories and poems, then started to write novels.

I was lucky – yes, I do believe in luck – to be able to reduce my work gradually over nine years following my husband's death. I had dreaded retirement but by the time it came I had written my first novel and was deeply into the second, exchanging a life of listening to stories for one of finding them inside myself.

Freud said 'The creative writer does the same thing as the child at play, he creates a world of phantasy which he takes very seriously while separating it sharply from reality... as people grow up they cease to play and they seem to give up the yield of pleasure which they gained from playing.' George Bernard Shaw developed this idea saying, 'We don't stop playing because we grow old. We grow old because we stop playing.'

I seem to have learnt to play again. The surprise is that I should discover this in my seventies. From my desk I watch the garden birds; three robins in a bush, one making a great fuss, a male perhaps, showing off? Jays, jackdaws, magpies, pigeons, even a sparrow-hawk. I no longer chase these predators away from the dunnocks and tits. They have to eat too. Pen in hand I write, cross out, transfer some words to the computer, delete and move. By midday I'm exhausted and have to distract myself until the next morning when my critical eye is refreshed and I find I have written rubbish.

The pleasure deepens as the characters take over. Descriptions become metaphors I have not seen. Following the advice of a literary friend I take up my poker and riddle the ash from the prose to try and make it burn more brightly. Each day I am aware of something new. I am reminded of an uncle, headmaster of a prestigious grammar school, who told his young staff 'teach something new every year, preferably something you know nothing about.' Learning and retaining new facts becomes more difficult with age but there are always new things to discover within oneself.

Ian Waring Green, writing in the Independent, says that 'natural curiosity is the prime force behind creative thinking and is something to be engendered in everyone, everywhere, whatever their age.' My hope for retired or older people is that they can find their own way to free their curiosity. Since my first novel was published I am aware that I shall never produce great literature. But, while joints and lungs and muscles shudder and groan, words re-arrange themselves and stories clamour to be written. I used to find facts boring, feelings and relationships were paramount. Now I chase knowledge, forget much of it and use less. But the world is a more interesting place as I search the Internet for gobbets of information, watch faces more closely, listen in to conversations, strive to imprint near and distant pictures on my mind. From my bed I watch the dawn begin to break. The interwoven branches of a tree contain a dramatic mystery. As the light strengthens, normality returns. Just occasionally a different perspective flickers at the edge of my sight.

I am tantalised by the possibility of moving out of the confines of my own skin, from behind my own eyes, to see the world from a new angle. But if I try to look more closely the vision vanishes.

My mother was a passionate atheist whose pride would never have allowed her to lean on any church whatever her despair. I think I too am an atheist, believing that we create our Gods, projecting our best and worst attributes onto them. But when the dark times threaten, when my luck runs out and there is not enough courage to face bodily pain or unbearable loss, I may need to turn to an 'out there' God. The generous Christians I have met encourage me to believe that, if I do turn to their God for help, even so late in life, my disbelief will be forgiven and I shall not be denied.

1996 . . . Six Years Have Passed

Now

Six years have passed. The tears well up
More slowly now, but still the source is deep
See both of us refracted through the distant years.
His puzzled manhood fractured in its prime
By the dissonance of war.
His stifled fears
Had shut an inner door.
But I was young and not so far from school,
I swam so happy in a shallower pool.
How could I hear the suffering poet call
For help to leave the horror?
To heal his troubled soul
And find a new tomorrow?
Yet from our different fates, we found a way
To travel our joint path, and stay together.
In me he found his innocence. I held
A man who kept his inner truth until the last
Until, six years ago
He slipped my grasp.

Then

He sends me the poems he's writing,
Of the fog and the chestnut trees;
The wren on the back of a farthing,
And the rain and the sun that he sees.
In Oxford he sits in his room
Full of hatred for man and his fate.
And he struggles to break through the gloom
Of "The years that the locusts ate".
He drinks coffee, and watches the High
As he waits for one friend to appear.
He's shut in, and out, as the people go by
And the ghosts of the past rumble near.
In a punt with the pole in his hand
Past loses the worst of its sting.
But what's left for this trained fighting man
Who can't kill the littlest thing?
There is judo and boxing and talk,
And a wish to repair the sad world.
There's a girl he can take for a walk
And a future that could be unfurled.

Is there a patient in the house?

Some four years ago, a good friend of mine told me he had just been to hospital. I enquired about his problem and was informed that he was quite fit, and his visit was to take part as a Simulated Patient for the Sheffield University Medical School.

Apparently, there are not enough 'real' patients in the Sheffield Hospitals to provide adequate training for the medical students at times of tutorials or examinations.

I expressed interest in this voluntary occupation. The next day a telephone call was received from the Clinical Skills Department of the Medical School confirming that I would like to take part as an acting patient. Thus began four years of a most interesting endeavour.

I well remember the first experience. This was an examination for the fourth year students. During the day about thirty students were to see me, together with an examiner. Each student had five minutes to attempt to carry out a diagnosis. The scenario given to me was that I had experienced stomach pains and went to hospital. Examinations were carried out and I was kept in hospital overnight. I was told that more examinations were required, and a further night's stay was needed. I was to refuse this suggestion, and was to say as strongly as possible that I wanted to go home. This refusal was to be repeated by me no matter how firmly I was told by the hospital staff. What the student did not know was that I was an alcoholic, as was my wife. After the five minutes were over the examiner asked the student the reason I wanted to leave the hospital. Almost all the students carried out this examination successfully. The fourth student and I recognised one another. She had no problem in discovering the reason why I refused to stay in hospital a further night. Ever afterwards my wife and I were known by his friends as the two alcoholics, and asked if we needed a drink!!

During the year there were approximately four tutorials and two or three examinationn. One of the tutorials, which I carried out several times, was to present myself wearing only trunks. Some of these tutorials took place in mid-winter, when it was very cold. On one occasion, this procedure was during a lovely warm day in summer. These teaching sessions were for junior medical students who had just completed anatomy and physiology, but had never experienced an examination of a 'live' person. A tutor and eight students came into the room and stood next to the bed on which I was lying. The tutor explained for about twenty minutes where the organs of the body were situated, and how to palpate them to ascertain whether there were any swellings. Each of the students then took it in turn to probe my body. This whole session took about an hour and a half, after which there was a break for coffee. The second session in the morning was with the same tutor and eight different students. I again listened to the same explanation from the tutor, and was handled by this new group of students. A break for lunch, and the same students, and the same speech, saw me lying prone and comfortable. After a while - I don't know how long - I was shaken, and awakened.

How embarrassing, but I hope I'm living it down!!

Some of the scenarios for the examinations require learning, but every session is most interesting and worthwhile, and I am pleased that I volunteered to take part in this activity for the medical students.

Retirement is part of life

The beginning

Born 25.01.29 Merthyr Tydfil, S.Wales. $1^1/_2$ lbs! Placed in a field in the early morning dew to give me more strength! Polio at 4 years old – throughout life it has been both a motivator and an inhibitor. The village was Welsh speaking; my father and mother kept the bakery and grocer's shop.

I was lucky to have super parents and the people of the village brought me up to 19 years of age. If I said to my father "I cannot do that" he would say "Have you tried – I will help you if you have tried"

These early lessons taught determination, the need to succeed in every endeavour, a hard but worthwhile early lesson.

I was bullied at school – the PT master taught me to box, provided I had a wall behind me or the ropes of the boxing ring – another lesson – defend yourself.

The first surgery on my gammy leg was at 14 years old – much improved – but over time it reverts to a less useful mode.

I was working with my father – his products were of very high quality – there was no challenge to me.

My surgeon provided a letter of introduction, i.e. a passport to any part of the hospital. A strong character said, "you are going to be a Radiographer like me". How could I argue? Many characters encouraged me; I remember them all with respect and thanks for their influence upon me.

The middle part

Leaving home, I went to Sheffield in November 1948 to study and qualify in Radiography. New people in a new place; standing on my own feet, I was again encouraged by kind people to continue to pursue education, singing solo and in a choir in Crookes Congregational Church and the Welsh chapel beneath the City Hall.

I thought in Welsh and spoke English in a large city far removed from Wales. "How green is my Valley" expresses much of feelings and emotions of those early years in Yorkshire. I got on well with these new people who spoke strange English with a direct honest approach to communication. Lessons from my youth supported me in this new environment.

My student friends keep in touch; my friends from home keep in touch with me. How good it was to have this support when my eldest son was killed.

My wife and I were students together and married in 1952.

We were unable to have our own children so adopted two wonderful sons in 1965 and 1966. These babies were our best and greatest gifts; we shall always love them without reservation. My eldest son is no more. Such sorrow which I cannot describe.

My younger son lives close by with his charming wife and our champion grandson who is 15 months old, a new joy, a new gift to treasure.

Life has taught us about love and sorrow.

Our professional careers developed, bringing us both much success, satisfaction and fulfilment. Early experiences reinforced our behaviour and progress in our adult lives. Does our DNA programme us? Are our pathways of life pre–determined?

My gammy leg continued to motivate and hold back progress, in the latter case as little as possible.

The last part

– retirement is enjoyed but age with its slowing effects is evident. My wife and I resist these effects by our combined determination to "keep going" and at the same time enjoying our shared experiences in retirement.

Questions arise which are difficult to answer. How long can we keep our property and large garden? How long will our health remain sound, both physical and mental? How will we cope when we are parted by death? These experiences and thoughts are new, we flounder to find solutions, my wife and I have very different views. How can we compromise to find acceptable answers and solutions to these pressing problems? We do not know, perhaps this is a solution in itself.

The challenges of old age are many. We do not what know what lies around the corner.

Our experience of life, of work, of retirement and old age is a journey preparing us to cope with dignity and purpose to the very end.

Things that go bump in the night

We probably spend about one third of our lives in bed. Going to bed and expecting and getting eight hours sleep is one of those delusions of old age.

Nights are regularly and frequently broken by visits to the loo, arthritic pains, alarming dreams, and insistent anxiety. Cramp, too, can be particularly vicious. The cramp that footballers get in the calf muscles is easily broken by the physio stretching the iron hard muscles in the opposite direction. Not so for us oldies for cramp affects muscle groups we never knew we had. Not only this, but it seems to be impossible to work out how to apply the counter stretch. Sometimes, and I don't really need to tell you, it can reduce you to a gibbering, groaning, swearing, helpless wreck. However, more commonly, cramp is brief and can be managed by getting out of bed, hoping for the best and getting back into bed very carefully, as your whole system seems to be on a sensitive trigger.

The natural history of cramp is not straightforward. You may be months without it and then for no apparent antecedent event it hits you again. You try Indian tonic water, salt solutions, hydration, magnesium, quinine from the doctor, counting backward from 100, praying, screaming and groaning. Cramp has a will of its own. I have come to the conclusion that it is something we are stuck with, just one of the challenges of old age.

We proudly invited my elderly parents to our first home. There was not much furniture so we bought a second hand double bed for them. There was a bump in the night. The box mattress fell through its supporting frame and tipped them on the floor. One wonders what had been happening and with such energy?

A few weeks later, a rather frail lady was sitting in the chair. She said she was not feeling too well; she had had a bad night. She went on to explain that the bed had collapsed. Her large Alsatian dog, seeking company, had leapt on her bed in the middle of the night bringing both of them to the floor. It was all sounding 'Thurberesque'.

A loud and sickening thud disturbed sleep. I got up, well armed with a poker, but no burglar. I found, at daylight, that the larger than life head clay had slid off its armature and hit the floor. It was a sorry and messy end to weeks of hard work.

Waking up in an intense sweat is not necessarily a sign of advanced tuberculosis. It is more likely to be a misalignment between you and the duvet.

Bodily contact is pleasant and reassuring. As for sex, well this happens occasionally but what do you expect when both partners are in their mid eighties. It's like Dr Johnson's remark on women preaching "It's not that it is done well but that it's done at all".

Valuable insights can happen at 3am. Maybe it is the solution to that computer problem that has worried you all day, a phrase or idea for your next publication or the name of a friend you ought to meet soon. This is fine but when half asleep between dream and reality it can get confusing. The intense embarrassment or anxiety in the dreaming state can only be shown the door by waking up fully and getting back to full consciousness. At a deeper level perhaps there is a real point in trying to understand these repetitive and nasty dreams. What are they trying to tell us?

All in all bed is a wonderful institution, well worth a third of our lives where we recover from the day and also have some varied entertainment.

From Ghoulies and Ghosties
And long leggety beasties
And things that go bump in the night
Good Lord deliver us.

Battered colander
– Father's Day –

A marvel, the battered and most ancient
Is put to use day after day for half
A century and six, the best design
Now without a handle, steam rises still
From cooked potato, bean and sprout drained and
Shaken, falling perfectly to table
Bowl: some brave soul fought against the tide of
Time and fashion preferring comfort and
Familiarity, to sexed up slick
Commodity thrown away when knocked and
Worn, but this battered colander remains
The best loved in all the world, working still
Serving, surviving the test of time - such
Clatter and crash each day, proof masterful
The father of all colanders valued
Above all

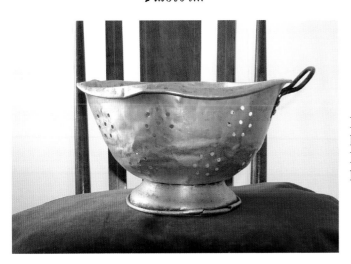

Don't ever underestimate the importance of money. I know it's often said that money won't make you happy. It's undeniably true but every thing being equal, it's a lovely thing to have around the house.

Groucho Marx

"How was it for you?"

The trouble with this simple question is that it isn't simple! In fact, unless I'm missing something fundamental, it is the most intrusive and personal question I've addressed today!

OK! Impersonal, if you don't know me/us; but pretty unveiling, if you do?

Anyway, in the interests of the greater good, here goes!

I think this will be a one sided response, since the wife cannot bring herself to write at the moment; but you never know.

I never gave retirement much thought until my wife took early retirement from teaching, which had been, for her, more of a calling than a profession. At one stage I expect she would have done the job for nothing, for the sake of the children, but in the end the unfairness of the system broke her. Other teachers were so unkind to her that she took early retirement. One new teacher was so completely disinterested in people, children, parents or staff, that when she came to work in the parallel class to my wife, the first thing she did was to slide the permanently open connecting door shut. She must have been in the job for the money. It certainly wasn't for the love of children! Her husband was a chief HMI, so it was no surprise when she eventually became head of the school.

My wife left as a disillusioned, sad teacher, whose career had begun so brightly with a distinction in classroom teaching. Perhaps she had been too naive. Nevertheless, her love for teaching and children continues to blaze, in contrast to what she feels is the cynical approach of the system combined with the attitudes towards her of apparent friends and colleagues who used the system to achieve their own success.

So, there we are! I would say that up until this point I had vaguely thought of myself as a sort of "Peter Pan". When asked when I thought I would retire I would generally answer, "I'll never retire!" Perhaps this was a way of avoiding the issue, but I think I genuinely did not imagine I would ever reach retirement age. It was something that happened to other people. Why on earth didn't I see it coming to me? And yet there had been tell-tale signs that were shouting at me. One was that I was finding it increasingly difficult to get through refereeing a soccer match without finding that at some stage in the game I could not keep up with play!

When the wife retired, she suggested that perhaps I might consider doing the same, even though I had 5 years to go, and then we could do things together. She had begun to find that, "solitary-confinement-retirement" brought its own difficulties and pressures. We decided that we would run with this plan if it was financially viable, and after investigation, I retired at 60. I would not do the same thing again. I had enjoyed the camaraderie of the staff room, but was never a natural teacher, so I had had to work quite hard in preparation and marking. I worked my socks off! This wasn't a problem initially; I was in it for the youngsters' benefit. My last Ofsted was a wake-up call because I had been working with the Deputy Head of the Grammar school for many years, he took some classes and I took others in the same department. He never did any marking and often I was in school 'til sunset, marking so that boys would always come in to up-to-date books. I was usually last out of school, setting the alarm before slamming the door behind me. I even spent hours painting pictures on the classroom walls to make the classrooms more interesting places for the boys to work in. The Ofsted inspector sat in on about 8 or 9 of my lessons and even came in on the Friday when, traditionally, "they" never come in! I had expected not to be visited for a 10th time so hadn't prepared much and had to wing it!" When our departmental briefing came around he was given, "excellent" and I was given "satisfactory". The main reason being that he discussed with the boys at length, and I "chalked and talked". Another tell-tale sign, showing that I was beginning to find it difficult to hear what the boys' responses were. Probably not bad enough to suffer the indignity of a hearing aid, but bad enough to make weekly discursive lessons rather difficult. I did feel that the assessment was unfair since it did not take any of my exhaustive overwork into consideration. I think that I had let work become more important than it should have been, or perhaps my traditional approach to teaching was being overtaken before my very eyes and I hadn't seen it happening. In fact, I was, "Out-of-the-Ark", and I hadn't realised it! IT and power point had arrived and I had not become aware of its significance. Actually, the fact that new technology had surrounded me without absorbing me into its brilliant new world of opportunities was another tell-tale sign that it was time for me to go.

So go I did!

I should have gone on a retirement preparation course or something like that, in order to open my eyes to just what "retirement" would involve. In fact, in my opinion, such courses can never actually demonstrate to the uninitiated the reality of retirement. It cannot be compared to any other experience, in that once you are in it, there is very little you can do to get out of it other than to make the best of it. It is a daily reminder that life and death are a reality and in fact, you are in it up to your neck!

If ever I had any doubts about my imminent demise, they are demonstrably exploded now! So, retirement for me has been coming to terms with the amazing fact that now I am 67 years old.

There must be some mistake, someone must be having a joke at my expense! How did it all happen? "Me, an old bloke?" Never!

As my old aunt put it, "I'm an 18 year old in an 85 year old body."

I try to keep myself fit by going out for "power-walks", but I must say I take a mobile phone, a couple of pounds and my bus pass with me, just in case.

I have found myself becoming somewhat unhealthily taken up with genealogy. I wish I had encouraged my parents and grandparents to talk. All the things that they knew, but of which they never spoke, and which I now wish I could relate to. Even though they are dead, I now find myself trying to experience their lives through the photographs and letters, fondly kept for so many years and now being deciphered by me as I try once again to get close to them. How much easier it would have been if only they had put names, dates, places on the backs of those black and white or brownish/sepia snaps.

Retirement would have been so much easier if we had prepared earlier for it. Money makes a great difference and those with a very small pension must find life so hard. If you've got a lot of disposable income, at least you've got a choice as to how to spend it.

I have always considered myself to be a fairly healthy person, so perhaps expected that to continue, in perpetuity. What a great surprise when life jumped up and kicked me.

Cancer of the bladder!

"Smoker?"

"Nope."

"Worked with rubber?"

"Nope."

"Just a bit of bad luck then."

All part of retirement's rich tapestry!

And then, being keen to keep fit, in spite of apparently dwindling returns, I decided to commit to a regime of "press-ups". Every day, starting with 10, I would do one more press-up every morning, on the bathroom floor, (where else?) before showering. Nobody would need to know, but would probably notice the youthful figure whilst swimming with the grandchildren.

All went well, first the press-ups, then the shower! Then for half-an-hour, no recollection of anything before finding the wife on the phone asking what she should do because I have been talking even more rubbish to her than usual. Asking why she's changed the room around and seeming for all the world as if I've had a stroke. Well, that took about a year to get to the bottom of. After being treated for TIAs, and going onto simva-statins and aspirins, a very well read young consultant (Yes, they really do all begin to look younger and younger!) listened intently to the symptoms.

He exclaimed, "I know exactly what that is, ischaemic global amnesia." When the arm muscles require more oxygen than usual and a particular part of the brain is starved of oxygen the subsequent memory loss causes, for instance, the "sufferer" to think that furniture in familiar surroundings has been rearranged.

No more press-ups! By order! But thank goodness it wasn't a TIA.

I think my old auntie's seen it for what it is. We stay the same person, basically, but have to come to terms with lots of life changes which we don't realise are happening to us until we are forced to face up to them. Retirement has forced me to address all kinds of changes that I thought were light years away, but have suddenly whacked me in the face!

As far as married life is concerned, everything is different now because we don't tend to take things as seriously as we may have done in the past. "Opposites attract", or so the saying goes. Unfortunately, as time goes on, we have found that this becomes less true. In fact our differences have become a source of great irritation and even of contention between us, so much so that if we had been well-off, we would have separated. But we can't afford to, so we have had to find ways of avoiding contentious issues. We try not to do or say things that we know upset the other person. We certainly have a mutual interest in enjoying our family and grandchildren. As long as we keep up our own interests to a certain extent, we don't seem to come up against each other quite as much. I can't say that it has been a great blessing to me to have to be at home with my wife all the time nor she with me, though sometimes it has been. Our lives seem to have been less difficult when we were out at work for most of the day, but as I say, as long as we have interests to absorb us for part of most days, we get by amicably. If we can do it, I should say most couples might be able to manage it.

We still sleep together, having put snoring to bed by means of a vertical piece of Boots micropore tape joining upper and lower lips. This is a brilliant way of permitting the sleeper to breathe either through nose or mouth if necessary without paying the earth for revolutionary, "snoring elimination devices". All kissing can be safely carried out prior to application of said tape and a quiet night is enjoyed by all.

My retirement so far!

I always joked that I would be well suited to retirement as I had so many interests other than work – DIY, cooking, house and garden, music, reading and walking. Now that I am retired, I am not disappointed. In many ways I am relieved not to be working, as the professional world is changing. In the last year or so it became more difficult keeping up with things generally and computers in particular!

I was a partner in a successful surveying practice and, when we sold out to an insurance company I worked for them for over three years. I found this difficult, as previously I had always been my own boss. However, having to move offices meant working with different colleagues, which I found stimulating.

My introduction to retirement was phased over two years, which worked well as there was no sudden break. My background was good – happy childhood, happy marriage and always reasonably well off.

I feel the success of my retirement was due to different interests, particularly a practical, hands on approach to things around the house and garden. I extended my interests by doing some voluntary work in the community and there was a gradual increase in social contacts. I also took a two year course in Photography at Sheffield College and I found it exhilarating mixing with other students, most of whom were much younger.

Looking back over the last twelve years I am not disappointed with my retirement. I find the most frustrating thing now is my lack of strength and energy in attempting jobs which I could do a few years ago, together with the ageing process – diminished hearing, eyesight and brain power.

In my retirement I have been very well supported by my wife and I try to support her. She tells me that I am becoming impatient which I know is true. On the other hand I am very tolerant of her foibles!

Sex in retirement

When we woke on a Saturday morning and might feel like making love, we sometimes noticed a silent small hunched figure in pyjamas against the central heating vent, quietly sucking his thumb. That was rather off putting. Or later we found that all teenagers in our house were regularly going to bed later than we were, so that any might come in and ask a question at any time. When they had all left, Granny came to live with us so a certain amount of freedom was curtailed

When we did actually retire we were on our own and did quite a lot of travelling. Sex became much more enjoyable in different places and settings.

We had sex on top of cliffs, in fields and woods and commons and even had it once in a spinney at the bottom of the garden where the wedding reception was taking place. We did not get caught as far as we know. We never quite managed it at 30,000ft up in an aeroplane. I believe you get a special title for that achievement. I, however, once got assaulted under a blanket when the lights were out in the middle of a night flight. That was by a professor who I did not know. He got his hand well and truly smacked and replaced. My partner was travelling first-class and I tourist! So even after retiral you can get interfered with.

After all this freedom the arthritis in my hands and wrists began to get worse. Who can have really enjoyable sex without using your hands as well as your body? I felt a bit resentful, but was firmly told that this is the way it is when you get older. Gradually I got used to the discomfort and the arthritis decreased slightly as time went on. But then a worse thing happened.

My partner went to the GP with a minor complaint. The GP decided to take his blood pressure. It was up, so drugs were prescribed. Exactly two weeks later he started having problems with sex never having had any difficulties before. Change of drugs made no difference. I felt cross that the GP prescribed NHS Viagra to men of 60 but not for my partner who was well over 70. This was a real case of ageism. However, when we tried over the counter Viagra, it wasn't much good anyway for drug induced symptoms.

Then in a real moment of love and consideration, my partner went into a sex shop with great embarrassment and bought a Christmas present for me of a silver friend with a battery. Used in mutual sex it gave me fantastic climaxes so that the end was better than at the beginning, for me at least. Now we are both a bit older. Bodily contact and snuggling up are both very enjoyable but the full works is much less often and we accept this. I think we are both fairly content. After all Abraham did it at one hundred years of age. Sarah doubted that he could manage it but she was proved wrong!

Lines written upon hearing the startling news that cocoa is in fact a mild aphrodisiac:

Half-past nine – high time for supper;
"Cocoa, Love?" " Of course, my dear."
Helen thinks it quite delicious,
John prefers it now to beer.
Knocking back the sepia potion,
Hubby winks, says "Who's for bed?"
"Shan't be long," says Helen softly,
Cheeks a-faintly flushing red.
For they've stumbled on the secret
Of a love that never wanes,
Rapt beneath the tumbled bedclothes,
Cocoa coursing through their veins.

What really matters

As the years slide by the sexual side of marriage diminishes in importance. What matters is companionship, remembering to put out the wheeley bins, repairing buttons and socks and picking things up from the floor; but none of these had loomed large in our selection of a partner.

Recycling life, finding and enjoying value

I had spent 30 years in a University medical practice and had never had a day off sick. A "health scare" led my medical children to point out to me that, contrary to my thinking, I was unlikely to live for ever and I should perhaps consider cutting down or even retire. The problem was, I enjoyed the medicine so much. I felt I was quite good at it by now, I was well qualified and having recovered from the episode after 6 minutes, I felt normal again. The fact was, however, that with changes in the practice, the National Health Service and the University, the demand as the Director of the service was becoming increasingly onerous, whilst resources were becoming less.

An opportunity arose where early retirement could be arranged for staff above a certain age with the option of continuing to work for 2 years and then being given added years to a pension. This sounded a good compromise – retire in two years' time as though I had worked longer as far as pension was concerned.

The option was in some ways attractive principally because I would have more time to spend travelling, with family and doing the things one never had time to pursue in a busy professional life..

I made the decision to accept early retirement on the basis that I could still practice medicine in a reduced capacity outside the confines of my longstanding practice as well as pursue new interests. I was, after all, spending a lot of time on committees (which I detested), writing papers for committees (which I also detested) and being the accountant, personnel officer for the staff as well as carrying a full clinical load.

I wondered if I would be missed and how I would cope without the stimulus of seeing young people with enquiring minds on a daily basis. I certainly did not want to leave with any fuss and refused a dinner by the chief executive, though the informal gathering sprung upon me by the staff in the practice, was memorable and was attended by invited guests from throughout the university.

The initial months of retirement were spent having a holiday in the south and acclimatising to a slower pace of life not having to meet deadlines at each hour of the day. This took some time to accommodate and I felt guilty at being able to sit down for an hour in the day to read the newspaper whilst trying to think what I would otherwise be doing at work.

It was not long, however, before I was telephoned by a practice in Sheffield, having heard that I had retired, requesting me to cover their surgery as a locum for a doctor's absence. I found this very agreeable, I was being useful again and being in demand. The demand for services grew and I found I had to restrict my availability as I was now 'retired' was I not? There was a difference in this sort of work – there was not the continuity of care that I had been used to giving, but I reckoned I could quickly get to the basis of many problems. Perhaps continuity of care was something I could sacrifice for my new found freedom.

I needed something to fill the gaps between the locum sessions and so I learnt computers at a course in Sheffield. This has proved very useful over the years both in locum practice and at home.

My father was a cabinet maker in London and I had inherited his tools. They lay untouched in his tool chest for 30 years apart from when our son wished to make something as a child or I had an urgent D.I.Y. job to do in the house. I have a great love of wood and fine furniture but my father's early experience in the 1930s' Depression in the trade in London led him to ban us from having anything to do with wood. He did however teach me how to French Polish when it was 'safe' that I was not going to be a woodworker.

What of these tools? Encouraged by a retired doctor friend who had taken up cabinet making, I started a

Community College course to do woodwork and found like minded newly retired men and women actually making some very fine pieces of furniture. With an excellent teacher, I made good progress and made some complicated pieces of furniture which were submitted for the City and Guilds certificate.

Having completed my last higher medical diploma at the age of 33, I vowed I would do no more exams. Even when I tried to relearn the piano, I refused to do the Grade examinations; but this was assessment not formal examination. I was delighted to be awarded the City and Guilds certificate. I now make furniture to commission and have done several pieces of restoration and repolishing. These pieces will hopefully outlive me and have produced tangible evidence for the family that I 'made things'.

I have been graced by good health up to now and a loving wife and family who have been very supportive. I still do some medical work and have often been asked by patients "are you a new doctor?" to which I reply, "no I am an old doctor being recycled". Recycling life is what retirement is about, I think; after the initial let down period, one finds a level at which to survive.

Good health and staying healthy is important but stimuli to the brain and a hobby to occupy one's interest, travel and one's family are sustaining.

The passage of time inevitably leads one to slow down and it is then that one wonders how one did a full-time job and all the other things one did in a busy professional life with a growing family of active children.

I consider myself extremely lucky – I did what I always wanted to do – to be a doctor. I was successful and at times unsuccessful. I look back at some of the people's lives that I influenced, most I hope for the better, perhaps some for the worse. Many are still in touch and have gone on to great achievements. Some still express their gratitude for what I did 20 or 35 years ago and are good friends, now all over the world. I was truly blessed and am ever grateful. I continue my locum work and my woodwork, my family are a delight, my wife a constant supporter.

From an early age I have felt a guiding spirit and my Faith has sustained me in all I have done. Could one be more grateful?

The old old song

When all the world is young, lad,
And all the trees are green;
And every goose a swan, lad,
And every lass a queen -
Then hey for boot and horse, lad,
Around the world away;
Young blood must have its course, lad,
And every dog his day.
When all the world is old, lad,
And all the trees are brown;
And all the sport is stale, lad,
And all the wheels run down -
Creep home, and take your place there,
The spent and maimed among;
God grant you find one face there,
You loved when all was young.

Charles Kingsley

Clergy wives

The retirement of clergy and their spouses varies in some respects from that experienced by others. They usually have to move away from the place in which they have been living and working for the past few years, thus losing home and friends as well as work. (Leaving Hathersage was particularly poignant for us, as we were so happy and had made such good friends there.) We have discovered that when one attends a church as a layman it is much harder to get to know people! On the plus side it was a relief not to have to try to live up to expectations parishioners might have of us – though this was less of a problem in Hathersage where relationships were on a more equal footing. Returning to Derby also had many advantages as we were able to reconnect to some extent with a former network of friends and acquaintances.

Since clergy do not have a very regular timetable and are usually in for meals anyway, adjusting to Jeremy's retirement was not a major problem, though living in a much smaller house does seem to mean that we are constantly tripping over each other or in each other's way. The usual chores and cooking still have to be done though we share these much more than formerly. This works well except when Jeremy tries to tell me how to cook something! I am still waiting hopefully for him to tidy his study! We still enjoy each other's company in bed from time to time [when we can stay awake long enough] and affectionate contact always.

I think it is important to have some separate interests, to give each other space. There is a danger in retirement of being together so much that we become perhaps too emotionally dependent on each other, knowing that one day we shall have to face separation by death.

I have found a relatively new interest in recent years in sewing and machine embroidery; attending classes in Nottingham has helped me to get out and about. Though now I feel perhaps I should be looking for something different to provide more local social contacts. Jeremy is much in demand for taking services in various parishes and occasionally at the Bridge Chapel (where we normally worship) or at the Cathedral. I am glad that he is still able to exercise this ministry and maintain contacts with people he knew in the past. For a few years I gave private lessons in German, but have given this up now, as I feel I am out of touch with the schools; sometimes I feel depressed by this loss of purpose.

Our family continues to give us both great joys and great sorrows. We are enjoying seeing our grandchildren growing up, but sad that sometimes our children have marriage problems. We enjoy visiting them all from time to time but are also glad to return home to peace and quiet!

Our caravan has enabled us to do quite a lot of travelling in Britain and on the continent, mainly in France, Austria and Italy, and we hope to continue this as long as we are both fit enough to do so. At the moment we are both still in good health, and count our blessings.

A change of view

I've always thought dependency
Might just show a tendency
Not to be an independent soul
But as the years tick by
And I become less spry
I might assume
A more dependent role
When well-meant help is offered
And timely support proffered
I'm learning to accept it with good grace
When the bookcase fell apart
A neighbour, bless his heart
Mended it
And stood it on its base
A lamb tumbled as it ambled
Got bogged down and tight-brambled
In the spillway underneath the bridge
I endeavoured to retrieve it
Struggled long, you must believe it
But had to phone a farmer
To pull it up the ridge
Then there was the beech tree
It fell to nearly reach me
In the strongest of the February gales
My heart was near to breaking
But this undertaking
Was all cut up and cleared
By a man from Wales
When I struggle with the shopping
With some limping and some lopping
An unexpected Sherpa is a blessing
So I no longer whine or whelp
I just accept the help
It's usually a man
– That's a bonus I'm confessing!

V. Jean Tyler in *'Survival, A Book of Everyday Verse'*

The tea dance

It's the Sunday tea dance and they'll all be here today,
Aches and pains forgotten, dance the afternoon away.
Foxtrots, waltzes, some are slow but some quite nifty,
With memories of how it was way back in 1950.
Norman's in the toilet and he's struggling to pee,
He's got trouble with his prostate and he'll likely miss
   his tea.
Eddy's got a new love that he met in Thornton Heath,
she does a lovely tango but she hasn't any teeth.
His latest fancy footwork nearly broke his partner's
   neck,
she mistook his outside swivel for a travelling contra
   check.
Ida's had her hair done and she's ready for the saunter,
but she had a vindaloo last night and it's coming back to
   haunt her.
Florry's mini-skirt's revealing when she's spinning in a
   jive;
she really shouldn't wear a thong approaching eighty-
   five.
They've had their tea and cakes and chat and had a little
   laugh,
and gamely rise with creaking knees to face the second
   half.
Norman's made it back in time for rumba number one,
his cucaracha's very neat but he's left his flies undone.
Vera's fallen over in a massive crimplene heap,
Bert's got indigestion and Mabel's fast asleep.
It's last waltz time and up they get for Humperdinck's
   old tune,
and then "goodbye, good luck, take care. God willing see
   you soon."

Anonymous

Notes to myself

Retirement may involve looking after an elderly relative; these few notes I made whilst trying to help my mother.

My mother was independent until she was eighty, then she gave up driving – "Difficult with a bad back", and gave up smoking – "Wasn't doing her chest any good".

I found it important that she felt she made the decisions, otherwise she became resentful.

Mobility

Stairs became a challenge and a hazard; "she" decided ground floor living was the answer. The dining room was made into the bedroom and an old pantry into the loo.

Arrangements

Treats, medical appointments etc. – keep it simple, only one thing each day. Always arrive on time and leave fifteen minutes to say goodbye – rushing off is a disaster. My mother enjoyed a pub lunch; we did a Derbyshire survey, and marked them out of ten!

The Dog

Something to look after and be responsible for. Mother had a dog called Whisky, they got old together. Eventually, a friendly neighbour came to walk her and stayed for glass of wine out of a box – easy to operate

Food

Eating was not a problem but constipation was. I encouraged her to have her main meal at midday and something light in the evening, a major change. Plenty of fruit and liquids – bitter lemon and a dash of gin certainly helped. As for shopping lists she had a pad and pen in the kitchen, bedroom and sitting room. Frozen meals were a godsend.

Domestic Help

We shut all the doors upstairs and arranged a cleaner for downstairs and help on bath days.

Telephone

In the bedroom and living room, they had large numbers and programmed buttons.

The Post

Mostly bills but I encouraged our boys to send postcards from their travels. She found a large spike easier than a clip and she gradually allowed me to take over the post.

Emergency Aid

A good idea but rarely round her neck.

Medication

My mother approved of the daily chart I made and enjoyed ticking it off in red.

Conclusion

I was well aware that I should encourage my mother's independence and not to take over too soon – also I had a life to live!

But she found that living became more and more of a struggle with good days and bad days. Money became an unnecessary obsession and general anxiety and worry about the world, listening to the radio news three or four times a day.

I think that it's inevitable that the nearest and dearest becomes the punch bag.

My mother died when she was eighty-seven after a year in a residential home. We had visited several (marks out of ten) and she decided which one to go to. Friends visited her for the first few months, then the family on alternate days. She was all there until a massive stroke one morning.

Beatitudes for the elderly

Blessed are they who understand
my faltering steps and shaking hand.

Blessed who know my ears today
must strain to catch the things they say.

Blessed are they who look away
when tea is spilled on the cloth that day.

Blessed are they with a cheery smile
who stopped to chat for a little while.

Blessed are they who never say
"You've told that story twice today".

Blessed are they who make it known
that I'm loved, respected and not alone.

And blessed are they who ease the days
of my journey home in loving ways.

Anonymous

In my new flat

In my new flat
I sat
No mail upon the mat
No ringing of the 'phone
I was alone

I went to church to see
Some company
A welcome was in store
I went some more
Is this what church is for?

But there's more good news
In the pews
Worship and praise
The good book says
No more lonely days.

Early learning

You soon discover:

That the toilet roll does not change itself automatically.

That it is genetically impossible to sit quietly while she parallel parks.

That you learn to be the ideal shopping companion.

That real men ask for directions when lost.

That learning to find things means looking in the right places and not turning the household upside down while screaming.

First things first

I can live with my arthritis
To my dentures I'm resigned
I can manage my bifocals
But – Oh God – I miss my mind.

Retiring and ageing

One of the things they didn't tell us about retirement was that the ageing process, which had already begun years previously, continues, slowly at first and then like time itself gradually accelerates.

On retiring with so much to do and think about, we have little opportunity to notice the minor aches and pains, which we all suffer from time to time. If we are lucky enough to have settled into a healthy and happy routine, retirement is wonderful and life is extremely good. Our life has become so full that we wonder "How on earth did we find the time to go to work". Hopefully we have a good social life surrounded and supported by many friends. We have joint interests with our spouses and our own separate interests. Some interests keep us physically fit, walking, swimming, gardening, dancing, fishing etc and other interests which keep our minds and brains alert and active.

Time passes, the ageing process still goes on and we find that our health suffers from the occasional hiccup. I have experienced some of these hiccups in the form of a hip-replacement, a heart attack which led to the necessity of undergoing a triple by-pass and two cataract operations. All of these operations have been dealt with very satisfactorily by the N.H.S. and I have come out a much fitter person. However, each time there has been a considerable amount of worrying about the operation, all of which was unnecessary because of the skills and techniques of modern medicine. As an aside my second cataract operation took just fifteen minutes to complete.

As we enter our seventies we find arthritic conditions, gradual loss of hearing and a general diminution of our physical abilities begin to occur; all of these we manage to cope with and life goes on. Life is still very good, and socialising with our peer group we find we are all more or less in the same boat.

The "crunch" comes when our spouses or we develop a condition that severely handicaps mobility or even worse when a dementia condition occurs. My wife, due to a previous back operation some years ago, has developed a severe pain problem in her lower leg. She needs to go regularly to the "Chronic Pain Clinic" at the Northern General Hospital. There they try one treatment after another to reduce the pain or help her to cope with it. She finds it extremely painful to walk any distance and so is unable to participate in what had been two shared interests, walking and dancing. She has persuaded me to carry on with these activities as she says they are good exercise for me. Although I do go from time to time, I do not enjoy them as much as I did and cannot help feeling guilty. While I am out having a good time, she is left at home on her own with the daily crossword, a good book or the television.

We discuss the problems and look at how we can resolve them, or at ways where perhaps we can improve things. An automatic gearbox in the car and a blue badge help tremendously with the "getting about" and enables my wife to attend meetings of the organisations to which she belongs.

These solutions are not a cure, and we are still left with two people, one who is in constant pain and has little mobility, and the other who is far more mobile. Both however are getting older and are slowing up. Occasionally this does lead to a certain amount of friction between the two, which is completely understandable. Most couples by the time retirement has progressed a few years and who have lived together for many years (fifty plus in our case), are able to surmount these difficulties because of the love for, and understanding of, each other.

Joint activities, not as strenuous as some previous ones enjoyed together, can be found. These are theatre, cinema and concert going, playing crib in a crib league and joining local groups and societies. The list can be endless and it requires a lot of will power and effort to do them, though it is well worth it in the end.

However, it is important that we still make time for our own particular interests.

Keeping in touch with our families and friends is also of great significance. I can always remember my mother saying to me "Time spent in pleasant conversation is never wasted." This saying has proved to be correct on so many occasions.

We are all different and have our own thoughts, attitudes and experiences. It is just possible that there is something to gain from others' stories?

Sandwich generation

This is something they don't tell you about retirement. Not everyone gets trapped in this concept but my wife and I are firmly entrenched.

So, how does this all work? It works by demand downwards (from parents) to needs (upwards) from adult offspring and their children. In our case it has meant a 25 year + support for one parent (97 years old) following widowhood and now failing health in sheltered accommodation, to the other surviving parent (nearly 97) now 10 years into widowhood, also in failing health in a residential home. The pressures are always there, from the basic requirement to visit on a regular basis, to crises in health, typically caused by falls, mini strokes and the list of supplementary ailments. Applying for assistance, dealing with support agencies, servicing the cost of residential care — all these elements come together to form a never ending menu of 'things to be done'.

On the other hand is the need to be supportive to your own offspring. We were the lucky ones, gone are the days of having careers and promotional aspirations with the same company for decades. In its place it's short-term contracts, applying for your own job, fixed rate mortgages that need to be re-negotiated. On top of this is the need to be a two parent 'earning machine'. Job satisfaction is subsumed by the need to service the pension contributions and try to find a way of getting off the treadmill.

Where did it all go wrong?

Back to the beginning?

Religious belief can be complex, personal, and difficult to write about, let alone read about! It tends to be grouped with politics and sex, as subjects not discussed in polite society. Even so belief or the lack of it appears to be important to many retired people.

So here goes! I propose to give a short account of my own background and then tell you about a major retirement project. Finally there will be a few speculative words about belief and old age.

The major influence in my young life was a boys' Bible class. It had a strong evangelical message. At the age of 12 or 13, I made a disturbing decision to follow Christ. There was a striking change of outlook which influenced major decisions in later career, marriage, military and professional life

As I grew older there was increasing difficulty with the paradoxes and concepts of religious dogma. The social and cultural baggage acquired became more and more uncomfortable and irrelevant.

Looking back, there have been many influences for change. Life events, meeting good men and women, many books, study courses, suddenly turning a corner and seeing a new vista and of course M's ideas, for she has moved on too.

Perhaps I should have accepted Sir William Osler's advice in *Science and Immortality:*

A perplexity of soul will be your lot and portion. Accept the situation with good grace.

Yes, I had an interesting, good and very 'successful' working life. A life that was blessed with change, opportunity and flexibility. The downside was that I was stuck with the paradigms of my Bible class days. At the same time I knew that there was much thought and hard

work to be put in before arriving at a more satisfying world view.

Being too busy, too tired, too idle, too distracted made it so easy to avoid this. Retirement came. No more excuses, this had to be my number one project. However, just before retirement, I wrote to a senior and much respected colleague to ask him how he was getting on. All his working life he had been extremely competitive and also competent enough usually to win. He had been capped several times for Scotland rugby, was a seriously good golfer and a dangerously funny after dinner speaker. This competitive stance was also a feature of his professional life. His reply said that in the early days of his retirement, he found himself sitting on the 18th green flooded in tears. He had played a poor game and there ensued almost two years of profound depression.

It seemed that his life and self-respect had been built on 'success.' Now he had failed at the last thing he was any good at. He eventually came to realise that in his intense desire to win he had neglected to build up his inner resources. I was certainly not free from my own quite different hang-ups. Perhaps I should seek help and clear some of the junk off my own deck before settling down to my primary project.

I spent an hour a week with a therapist in a downtown garret for six months. It was far too pleasant. There was no challenge and no blood on the carpet. After six months I was getting nowhere. Later, I consulted a Psychiatrist and Psychotherapist all rolled into one. After the first hour he wryly told me that I was not certifiable! He put me on a course of cognitive therapy for self-esteem. I really tried but ended up by being irritated and cynical of the method. These two excursions into the psyche were, for me, an expensive dead loss as far as retirement preparation went.

To help the main project I tried to find a spiritual adviser. The relationship broke down when he suggested that I should start learning New Testament Greek! So it was now down to me, with no further delaying tactics, to try to find out what I really believed. What was baby and what was bath water? A huge and probably impossible task on which to embark.

A year's University course on the philosophy of religious language followed by a year blundering about in the mysteries of Wittgenstein proved a major turning point. Heavy reading included the splendid Hans Kung, Joseph Campbell, Karen Armstrong, Paul Tillich, John Henry Newman, Richard Holloway, John Spong, John Hick, James Atkinson and over and over again, since the age of 45, Karl Rogers On Becoming a Person.

There was a year's course occupying seven hours a week on the structure and writing of the Old Testament which made for an about turn in attitudes to the Bible.

Retreats and discussion groups ranging from the 'Cutting edge of Theology' to 'New ways of seeing and feeling' and the concept of a 'thin place' – formed a major part of the search.

I found myself more and more suspicious of religious people or atheists who had "arrived" and knew they were right.

The following two quotations were encouraging:

Our greatest truths are but half-truths. Think not to settle down forever in any truth, but to use it as a tent in which to pass a summer night, but build no house on it, or it will become your tomb. When you first become aware of its insufficiency, and descry some account of truth looming up in the distance, then weep not, but rejoice: it is the Lord's voice saying, "Take up your bed and walk".
(Arthur James Balfour, 1848 to 1930, a politician later to become Prime Minister of Great Britain)

The scientist who developed the Saturn 5 rocket that launched the first Apollo mission to the moon put it this way:

You want a valve that doesn't leak and you try everything possible to develop one. But the real world provides you with a leaky valve. You have to determine how much leaking you can tolerate.
(Obituary of Arthur Rudolf in The New York Times Jan 3 1996)

After this entire hotchpotch over the years where am I? A few bullet points might help to indicate the sort of changes that are happening.

- Past dogmatism has faded. I know, I know, less and less. The value I used to place on words and formulations is downgraded.
- Words separate us from the animals and are a human glory. Words, however, are dangerous and should carry a health warning.
- Words are slippery and fallible and should be held lightly. Taking words seriously has been at the bottom of many persecutions, revolutions, wars, terrorist movements and family quarrels.. The pretence that words mean what they say is demonstrated in many diplomatic communiqués, political spin and some religious creeds.
- 'God' must be 'other'. As Christians what do we really know? According to the writer of Hebrews --- something from the Prophets and ultimately in the incarnation of Jesus. Even then we can only can get

such glimpses, as humans are capable of perceiving. Most of this is wisely communicated in metaphor and parable. How can we be dogmatic about theological matters when the knowledge of God is so very partial? How can we use those slippery words to encompass the indefinable? You really should not go to the stake for words. Both parties to any dispute, whether it be industrial or theological, must work to identify the emotional and motivational content which lies behind the words. This takes a lot of time and a lot of humility – both in short supply!

- The Science and Religion debate has become a bore.
- If the logical positivists wish to define what is valid in a precise and certain manner, so be it. That is their game and their rules and they are at liberty to play it. However it does seem to be arrogant and at variance with the facts of life. To hold that objective observation, the weighing, the measuring, the logic and deduction are the only avenues to truth and wisdom. Music, Art, Poetry, Religious experience are all part of a bigger picture.

There is a well used quote from *The Rock* by T.S. Eliot.

Where is the Life we have lost in living?
Where is the wisdom we have lost in knowledge?
Where is the knowledge we have lost in information?

The problem of evil and suffering is firmly faced in the book of Job. Maybe it is a problem if we carry a distorted view of God.

The Incarnation and the Resurrection carry huge implications. The stories are told in the language and perceptions of the time. Concentration on the implications behind these descriptions might be more profitable than getting stuck in the words.

That's enough about my major retirement project. Has this sort of journey anything to do with the process of ageing? I started this journey mainly as a cerebral exercise but I suspect that getting old of itself has accelerated my changes in outlook.

The enthusiasms of younger life, the drive, the dogma,

the certainty of purpose all tend to fade whether this is in religion, idealism, politics, profession or business. Detail becomes of less importance, whilst the underlying principles remain strong and simple. Perhaps we are moving full circle back to the simplicity, the wonder, and the humility of ourselves when very young. Is T.S.Eliot saying something like this in *Little Gidding*?

We shall not cease from exploration
And the end of all our exploring
Will be to arrive where we started
And know the place for the first time.
Through the unknown, remembered gate
When the last of earth left to discover
Is that which was the beginning.

So I may have been wasting my time. Advancing years alone might have naturally brought me to a similar outlook?

I was fascinated to come across this piece by Carl Jung. It may ring a few bells for you too.

And so I am disappointed and not disappointed. I am disappointed with people and disappointed with myself. I have learned amazing things from people and have accomplished more than I expected of myself.

I cannot form any final judgement because the phenomenon of life and the phenomenon of man are too vast .

The older I have become, the less I have understood or had insight into or known about myself.

I am astonished, disappointed, pleased with myself. I am distressed, depressed, rapturous. I am all these things at once and cannot add up any sum. I am incapable of determining ultimate worth or worthlessness. I have no judgement about myself or my life. There is nothing I am quite sure about. I have no definite convictions - not about anything really. I know only only that I was born and exist, and it seems to me I have been carried along .

I exist on the foundation of something I do not know. But in spite of all uncertainty, I feel a solidity underlying all existence and a continuity in my mode of being.

From *Memories, Dreams, Reflexions*, by Carl Jung

You may find the following piece by Francis Kilvert to be soothing and satisfying. The top and tail is by Thomas Merton:

The capacity to be still, to listen and to wonder, is illustrated by such reflective characters as Francis Kilvert, Curate in South Wales in the 1870s. He goes into Clyro Churchyard:

'After luncheon I spent a happy half-hour in the lovely warm afternoon wandering about Clyro churchyard among the graves. I sat awhile on the old Catholic tomb of the relict of Thomas Bridgwater under the South Church wall, near the chancel door. This is my favourite tomb. I love it better than all the tombs in the Churchyard with its kindly Requiescat in Pace, the prayer so full of peace.... A small and irreverent spider came running swiftly towards me across the flat tombstone and scuttling over the sacred words and memories with most indecent haste and levity. Here it was very quiet and peaceful, nothing to disturb the stillness but the subdued village voices and the calling of the rooks nesting and brooding in the tops of the high trees in Castle clump. Somewhere near at hand I heard the innkeeper's voice behind the church and across the brook giving orders to a workman about planting some quick and privet.'

Here is a man, albeit from a previous century, sitting quietly and uncovering the silence. In that peace he fills the

space with a depth and quality which shows up the way that our indulgence in busyness leaves us with shallowness in life. He makes space and time for the peace of God to reach him.

Pre-retirement

Coming up to 83 as I am it may be time to talk about retirement, but first a few thoughts about what has been going on since my first 'Job Change' in 1987. Till then I was Professor of Psychiatry at the University of Sheffield, though I had been spending occasional periods with the Department of Health working as a medical member of a team in the Hospital Advisory Service, a group set up by Richard Crossman in 1970 to monitor Services for Mental Illness, Mental Handicap and the Elderly in hospitals in England and Wales; he described it in his Memoirs as one of the two best things he did as Secretary of State for Health.

In 1987, I was offered the post of Director of the renamed Health Advisory Service, and as at that time I was over 60, I resigned from the University, telling them I would not return at the end of the 4 years. I retained my house in Sheffield, leaving Renée to hold the fort, while I swanned off over the country, spending two to three weeks at various centres looking at their services and 'Reporting to the Minister' - one Edwina Currie. At the end of my Directorship, I retired to my home in Sheffield, there to offer to do a locum psychiatrist post for 6 months while they found a full-time Consultant - that lasted three years, and a busy time too, as drugs and alcohol services are not the quietest and well staffed of the psychiatric activities.

However, things would have gone well, except that, while participating in another of my extra-mural activities as external examiner in psychiatry at the University of Singapore every August, in 1990 Renée and I went on our usual jaunt - we had been going for about five years at that time, but to my great surprise, she started complaining that she did not like the food, and could not eat very much - quite out of character compared with our previous visits. As soon as we got home, she was investigated, operated on for carcinoma of colon, and by May of the following year she was gone.

Looking back on the event, it is difficult to know what to say. It was all very rapid, with my dearest disappearing before my eyes, except that with her failing liver, she was also getting immobile with oedema. She stayed at home till two days before she died, when she was admitted to St Luke's Hospice, where she had worked as secretary to the Matron for a number of years, and said as she came in 'It's like coming to a party of old friends.' But alas, for only two days, when she suddenly stopped breathing.

My daughter, Sharon, went back to her home in London - Renée had three pregnancies, Sharon and two ectopics - and I returned to my work, which was a valuable opportunity to keep busy for a further couple of years. Bereavement is a very personal experience, one that is difficult to share with other people although in general, all one can say is that it leaves an enormous gap, which has to be filled, one way or another. Each has their own way, and it is not something you can practise in advance, and I am not sure it is something that other people can usefully advise you about, because everyone's circumstances differ. One of the most difficult circumstances I found I had to cope with was managing other people's embarrassment when they sailed up to me in the street and asked: 'How's Renée?' It is these small matters that are difficult.

Eventually, they appointed a new consultant for drugs and alcohol and I had my third retirement - well, sort of! Because one of the multifarious tasks required by law for people suffering from serious mental disorders was to have a legal process available to control admission and discharge of disturbed individuals from hospital and other forms of care. This meant that a complicated system of supervision had to be available to ensure that such people were fairly and appropriately treated, and their rights, and those of the population at large, protected. One aspect of this was a system of Mental Health Review Tribunals to which patients and their relatives could appeal to ensure that any detention was legal and appropriate. The Tribunals, regionally organised, consisted of a legal member chairing, with a psychiatrist and a lay member, often from social services, hearing these cases, listening to the patient, usually legally represented, and the supervising hospital with information from appropriate members of staff.

Membership of these Tribunals involved travelling to different parts of the Region, as a psychiatrist examining the patient, often talking to relatives and members of staff, and then sitting as a tribunal member to make a decision about detaining or discharging the patient concerneed. This work kept me reasonably busy until I got a letter informing me that my membership could not be renewed when I reached my 75th birthday. I appreciated that by that age, some people may be a little uncertain about their memory and judgment generally, so when I wrote to the Lord Chancellor and the Prime Minister complaining about this decision, I suggested they may wish to contact various colleagues who had been sitting with me to ensure my decisions were sound. I was told that although they were desperate for psychiatrists there could be no exception to the decision as there had been a regulation established forbidding membership of any judicial proceedings over the age of 75, and as I understood it, this was because there had in the past been difficulties about certain very elderly judges who had passed their prime. So here I was, having reached my fourth retirement, unemployed and unpaid.

Fortunately, marriage summoned me, to a widowed lady who had been a friend of Renée and whom I had of course known; we had also known her late husband. She certainly filled the unemployed gap, though not the unpaid part, but my pension was at hand to deal with that important aspect. So getting together, finding a joint house, meeting all her family - she has five children and fifteen grandchildren - offered ample activity for the time being.

However, not because I was bored, but because I was interested and she as a sculptor, also had her 'off-duty' activities, I decided on an Open University course in Humanities, largely guided by her advice, or I might otherwise have gone into psychology or sociology, linked with my former role; this would have been a grave mistake - maybe literally. I completed this with an Honours B.A. and proceeded further in looking at Madness and Shakespeare, something which now fills my occasional leisure time. The OU was an interesting experience, and should certainly be considered by anyone looking for stimulation and studying in a welcoming environment - many were middle-aged+ ladies who had lost out on previous opportunities when younger and found this a valuable method of developing a new brain-stretching activity, when freed from family responsibilities.

I do have some spare time, which I spend walking with a couple of groups in the Peak District, and I also act as a simulated patient for the medical students, who nowadays cannot rely on spending enough time with real hospital patients who whistle through so quickly that they have no opportunity to talk to anyone, certainly not medical students. I also keep in contact with the National Health Service in my role as elected Governor for the Sheffield Teaching Hospitals Foundation Trust, in which role I have still two years to go before I reach my fifth, or is it sixth retirement.

So I do believe in retirement as long as one keeps on doing it regularly!

A ninety something looks back

What a thought! I have been retired for one third of my life! With hindsight, down a viewpoint of ninety plus years, it has worked out well. We retired to Grindleford, so close to our home in Sheffield. We were able to keep up with our old friends and make new ones.

The good folk of Grindleford were very friendly and invited us to join in village life. Before long we were involved in the Horticultural Society, Parish Council, Methodist Church, CPRE, Probus, Hope Valley Rail Users and more. We enjoyed our sixties, still full of beans and thrilled to be living in such a beautiful place.

My husband and I had a marriage of equals. We rarely quarrelled and we helped each other in many projects. I remember one Parish Council AGM; the Chairman asked my husband why he had come. He said 'I come as Mrs. Foster's spear carrier!'

The week my husband retired from the Civil Service, he was invited to join the board of a building society. This meant he went to town two days a week. This eased him into retirement. He went around with a smile on his face for seventeen happy years.

Since he died, I have had to come to terms with loneliness. I keep my best photos in glass fronted cupboards in my line of vision and often have a word with my mother, my father, my husband Maurice and my son Murray. I also talk to myself. It's ok; there's only me listening!

I think we are very fortunate today in our old age. What price the telephone and the TV?

Even in the middle of the night there are interesting programmes for insomniacs. The Radio Times sorts the wheat from the chaff.

It helped me to be involved with the Methodist Church. I like the sort of people who take the trouble to support the local church. I have belonged to eleven churches in England, Scotland and Wales. The present one is the best ever, possibly because I have plenty of time nowadays. Members vary in their beliefs, which we rarely discuss. We sing all the old hymns with gusto. The music is inspiring and the words poetic and this is our Christian heritage.

Being able to drive is a huge benefit. Many women who were content to let their husbands do all the driving, are in a fix when they are widowed. My husband insisted that I learned to drive in my fifties and thank goodness he did. I am now much in demand for lifts (only locally of course).

Approaching retirement I used to plan to study sundry courses, car maintenance etc. In the event I managed one, chair repairing at Hope Valley College. We were so involved with the village that time just flew happily by.

Gardening has always been one of my enthusiasms but its days are gone. Now I am only good at pruning and have to ignore most weeds. If I get down I can't get up! It's a good idea to simplify the garden before you get too decrepit. For instance my gardener (of 25 years service) and I removed two large rock gardens, levelled and grassed the area with snowdrops in the turf of one and crocuses under the other. We also dug up old rose beds and grassed them. Much to the delight of the neighbours, eight cupressus were dug up by the roots.

A lifelong keen reader, the sixties and seventies gave lots of scope. A novel and more serious reading were always on the go, but fading vision has put the damper on that. What next? Well, radio of course, a whole new area for me to explore.

I thought time would go slower as you became old, but forget that. It seems to go quicker. Of course you have to fit in time for catnaps and larger naps and daydreaming

My father's comment on retirement was 'I don't know how I ever found time to go to work'.

Words of warning:

Don't get overloaded with good works. These are golden years. It's a shame to get stressed.

Beware of acquiring too many possessions, they all make for extra work.

Don't leave things too late. There is a tendency for "can't be bothered" to set in when you get to eighty.

Feeling at ease with retirement

It is 22 years since I retired and I have found the years enjoyable with no problems or regrets. The move into retirement was possibly made easier by having a 5-year, 2 days a week consultancy after retirement, which I referred to as a 5-day weekend. In my view it is too late to start thinking about retirement when it is rapidly approaching. In fact I think that there are several stages in life that need careful thought and planning. These stages can be considered as:

The Education Years - to 25
Marriage and Family Years - 25 - 50
Post-Family Years - 50 - 65
Retirement - 65+

The Marriage and Family Years are very full for both husband and wife but the Post-Family Years, after the last child has left for University, are as much a challenge (and hopefully an opportunity) as Retirement. This is the time, when other activities should be developed, which can then lead on smoothly into retirement.

Part of my reason for feeling at ease with retirement was that I had achieved all of my ambitions in my professional life. Another reason was that there had been a marked change in the industry that I worked for. We had spent 30 years building up the company to be a world leader, but from 1980 onwards there was contraction, plant closures and manpower reduction, with all the management time that this requires. This is dispiriting work

I felt no loss of status on retirement. My work has been published and was well-received. It is included in text books so will be around for some time ahead. I have been asked what I miss. Certainly I miss the close interaction with colleagues and the pleasure from seeing a project successfully completed or a problem solved. What I do not miss are the endless meetings and bureaucracy of a large company, the early morning train to London, or the secretary's voice saying the Chairman is on the phone.

I cannot say that there have been any problems in living in close proximity to my wife. She has a wide range of outside activities, far more than I have, whilst I value being able to devote as much time as I like to the activities that I enjoy. My professional life involved a lot of reading and study in depth, which I have continued over a wide range of subjects.

We made a big effort to keep a structure to our lives. For example, we make sure that our weekends are different to weekdays, so that there is a form to the week. We plan holidays and visits to relatives so that these are spaced out during the year, giving a form to the year. It is the freedom to arrange our activities in the way that we wish, and as frequently as we wish, that convinces us that retirement is great!

Retirement ~ a woman's thoughts

Retirement for me was never an option. It is a name given to time floating from here to there, a freedom with no strings attached. So where do we begin?

Could I really do whatever I chose? I was fit, eager and "yes" excited, but did I really have total freedom? Almost, providing that my dearest one and I agreed. A work and play partnership was formed quite accidentally and it appeared that a new and exciting time was about to evolve.

But did I want to plan an ordered, workable programme? Surely this could be a "shadow" of my working life. The sense of "freedom" appears to be disappearing. Nevertheless, the choices are there to take – no hurdles to jump over; no others to intervene. Freedom is really mine!

To be able to use this precious time of our lives is indeed a great privilege. Family and life-long friends can share the joy with us. The journey has now taken place and I thank God that our children and their children have been very much involved in its making. As we gather the "age" years, we also gather health problems, but these must never be allowed to mar our life-style because they were never in our original programme.

"Retirement" – Just the finale to a contented and active life-style!

There's that "You're only as old as you feel", which is fine to a point, but you can't be Shirley Temple on the good ship Lollipop for ever. Sooner or later, dammit, you are old.

~ Joan Crawford

Old age is like everything else. To make a success of it you have got to start young,

~ *Fred Astaire*

The computer swallowed grandpa

The Computer swallowed Grandpa.
Yes, honestly it's true!
He pressed "control and "enter"
And disappeared from view.
It devoured him completely,
The thought just makes me squirm.
He must have caught a virus
Or been eaten by a worm.
I've searched through the recycle bin
And files of every kind;
I've even used the Internet
But nothing can I find
In desperation I asked Jeeves
My searches to refine
The reply from him was "negative"
Not a thing was found "online".
So, if inside your "inbox"
My Grandpa you should see,
Please "copy", "scan" and "paste" him
And send him back to me.

Old age

Whenever I meet him I utter a curse
For he bores me to death reciting his verse,
When he's finished with that it's the family tree
Which of course I really do not want to see.
He forgets what he's said and repeats himself twice
Telling jokes which are corny and not very nice.
Embarrassed, my wife is reluctant to spend
More time with him than an infrequent week-end.
We continue to visit this man, but it's sad
To see how old age is affecting my Dad.

Schulz philosophy

The following philosophy has been commonly and wrongly attributed to Charles Schulz, the creator of the 'Peanuts' comic strip. The author's name is not known.

You don't have to actually answer the questions.

1. Name the five wealthiest people in the world.
2. Name the last five Heisman trophy winners.
3. Name the last five winners of Miss America.
4. Name ten people who have won the Nobel or Pulitzer Prize.
5. Name the last half dozen Academy Award winners for best actor and actress.
6. Name the last decade's worth of World Series winners.

How did you do?

The point is, none of us remember the headliners of yesterday. These are no second-rate achievers.

They are the best in their fields.

But the applause dies.

Awards tarnish.

Achievements are forgotten.

Accolades and certificates are buried with their owners.

Here's another quiz. See how you do on this one:

1. List a few teachers who aided your journey through school.
2. Name three friends who have helped you through a difficult time.
3. Name five people who have taught you something worthwhile.
4. Think of a few people who have made you feel appreciated and special.
5. Think of five people you enjoy spending time with.

Easier?

The lesson:

The people who make a difference in your life are not the ones with the most credentials, the most money, or the most awards. They are the ones who care.

After retirement – what?

I feel that I have had three different lives.
- Preparation, which includes birth, childhood and adolescence.
- Adulthood, the world of work and family.
- Retiral, with our children now independent, the growing awareness our own bodily deterioration and finally death.

We see death all around us, in many cases it turns into new life. The leaves fall and then the buds fatten and new leaves eventually grow. We plant seeds in the garden and as they die new life appears, a flower, a vegetable or perhaps a tree. Why should it not be the same for us?

When I was very ill at 14 with typhoid fever and being nursed at home, I overheard my father telling my siblings to be quiet as I might die. I felt quite calm about this and I was not afraid of dying because I believed that God loved me and that I was in his care. I knew the 23rd Psalm in the Old Testament in which David said, *"When I walk through the valley of the shadow of death, I will fear no evil as Thou art with me."*

I did not think about death much when I was young with all of life before me, except to hope that my parents would not die until I was independent. I did later also hope that neither my husband nor I would die till our children could fend for themselves. I was shocked when I met a young woman of 30 who had three small children and who had cancer of the breast and secondaries.

Now in our retiral I have had more time to think about it, I find that I quite look forward to the adventure of dying and going into a quite different existence. What I am afraid of is mental deterioration and being a real nuisance to my relatives.

What grounds have I got for feeling that after death

there is something lovely and wonderful. In the Bible we are told that *"Eye hath not seen nor ear heard nor hath it entered the heart of man the things that God has prepared for them that love Him."*

(*1 Corinthians*, Chapter 2 verse 9.)

When we die God will give us a lovely new body, just the kind that He wants to have. It will be a spiritual body, perhaps with a blueprint of our individual DNA. It tells you all about it in *1 Corinthians*, Chapter 15 verse 35 to the end. The Living Bible makes it clearer:

"We know that there is such a thing as a spiritual body as Jesus rose from the dead and there is historical evidence for this, He had a body not like ours. He passed through walls when the disciples were in a locked room, very frightened of the Jewish leaders. Jesus appeared more than once in these circumstances. The disciples were filled with joy instead of cowering and terrified. Something must have caused this change and made them bold."

(*Gospel of John*, Chapter 20 verse 19.)

Even in the Old Testament people realised that we were not just physical but had spiritual qualities;

"Love is strong as death. Many waters cannot quench love nor floods drown it."

(*Song of Solomon*, Chapter 8 verse 6.)

Surely these spiritual qualities in us will survive our bodily death and will not be snuffed out?

I am not ready for death yet, as there is a lot more that I want to do, and I do not want to leave my husband, our children and grandchildren yet. I am also looking forward to seeing our great grandchildren.

I live in hope for the future, not certainty, but strong hope, that when I die I will be with God, because of His love for all of us, shown in Jesus Christ.

Bereavement and after – or life after death

In 1990 I decided to retire from work, partly because I felt it was the right timefor me to do so, but primarily because my lovely, slim, energetic wife, four years my junior was to undergo open heart surgery and I wished to be available to assist in her recovery.

The operation was a success and she worked extremely hard to recover full fitness. I was reasonably fit and active but she could soon out-walk me, even downhill.

We greatly enjoyed our retirement until, three years down the line, following investigation and some surgery we were given the shocking news that she had cancer of the liver and had only a short time to live.

I looked after her at home with the wonderful help of our GP and a McMillan nurse. I will not enlarge upon the trauma of those mercifully few weeks or the ensuing grief. It was not until after the funeral that the enormity of my loss really struck home. I had always regarded myself as being a self-sufficient type and I was not afraid of my own company. When my children and close relatives and friends eventually left me to my own devices, at my insistence, I fully realised how achingly lonely the life of a new widower can be.

I even questioned my own need for survival in what seemed to be a pointless existence. I have no religious faith to fall back on but the idea of voluntarily giving up life had no appeal, especially when I considered the effect on my son and daughter and a few others. It also helped that I am a devout and practising coward! I did not feel the need for outside help and realised my salvation would have to come from within.

My wife was avery practical and positive person and I wondered what she would have said to me. It would have been along the lines of: "Come on now, darling. Pull your socks up and get on with it. Start now!" She had even remarked on one occasion that she hoped I would be able to enjoy the rest of my life and that she had thought of her replacement. I felt that was an utter impossibility and she never told me just who she had in mind!

I decided that I had to keep busy – apart from gardening, shopping , laundry, cooking for one, some entertaining and general household tasks. I went to evening classes in Art and French conversation. I joined a Bridge group and an Art Club. I was introduced to the noble game of crown green bowls at which I made some great friends such as Guy and took up snooker.

Of very great benefit however was the fact that the Probus Club was just getting going and I made many new friends there such as Ben, Ed, George, Maurice F, Bob, Wynford and Ryland. It was Ryland who insisted that I join the Committee as Treasurer, assuring me that the Club might have to fold if I did not take the post. I didn't fall for that line but I took the job, albeit with some reluctance and initial invaluable help from Les.

I served in various capacities on the Committee for some nine years and brought about some mutually useful cross-fertilisation between Baslow Bowls Club and Hope Valley Probus, making other friends along the way, such as several Ians.

Best of all was that I started to take holidays abroad again in the USA and Europe, with old friends. It was on a holiday at a large hotel in Southern Spain that a vivacious, charming lady, surrounded by admirers, was pointed out to me by the couple I was with. When I could get near I struck up a conversation and discovered that, although she now lived in Sunning Hill, this lady had been brought up in South Yorkshire and as children we lived within sight of one another. We knew many of the same places such as Millhouses and Ladybower. I was not looking for a new relationship and had reconciled myself to a solitary old age. This was like meeting up again with a dear friend and we got on remarkably well right from the start. We made the best of the three days left of my holiday, exchanged letters on our return home, and then visits. She was welcomed by my family and everyone who got to know her. She had been a widow for eighteen years when I met her. We have been together for over ten years now. She shares many of my interests and has some of her own. To say that she brought enjoyment back into my life would be a considerable understatement!

It is commonly said that time heals everything. That is not altogether true. With the passage of time one learns to cope with a new way of life and nature seems to aid in this by allowing memory to be selective of the happier times whilst dimming the sorrows . It also helps if you take on as many new projects as you can so as to broaden the options which thereby present themselves.

Advice from a South African friend

I hope you stress the necessity for retirement planning for your male colleagues, who don't often have hobbies to which they can turn.

Many of my male associates were workaholics and

a. Did not want to retire

b. Hadn't any alternatives to their medical research work

c. Whose wives point blank refused to have them hanging around the house all day and waiting for a three-course lunch

Now that Wits is making 60 years their obligatory retirement age, it will be even worse!

"No Spring, nor Summer beauty hath such grace,
As I have seen in one Autumnal face."

The Autumnal, John Donne

Fear no more . . .

Fear no more the heat o' the sun,
        Nor the furious winter's rages;
Thou thy worldly task hast done,
        Home art done, and ta'en thy wages:
Golden lads and girls all must,
As chimney-sweepers, come to dust.

Fear no more the frown o' the great;
        Thou art past the tyrant's stroke;
Care no more to clothe and eat;
        To thee the reed is as the oak:
The Sceptre, Learning, Physic, must
All follow this, and come to dust.

Fear no more the lightning-flash,
Nor the'all-dreaded thunder-stone;
Fear not slander, censure rash;
Thou hast finished joy and moan:
All lovers young, all lovers must
Consign to thee, and come to dust.
No exorciser harm thee!
Nor no witchcraft charm thee!
Ghost unlaid forbear thee!
Nothing ill come near thee!
Quiet consummation have,
And renownèd by thy grave!

William Shakespeare, *Cymbeline*

Facing death

In the Old Testament, Ecclesiastes says there is a time to be born and a time to die. The former we have all undergone without memory or experience, but the latter is still ahead ... time and date unknown. For most of us it is usually on our mental back-burner. We prefer not to think about it. It is something which is hopefully years ahead, and we prefer not to think about it NOW.

There are times, however, when death strikes suddenly, and without warning.

Although in life we have obviously mourned the deaths of family members, friends, and, sadly, children, arguably, the saddest and most poignant death of all is the sudden death of one's marriage partner.

One can never prepare for the feeling of utter grief, loneliness, bewilderment, and even anger, when one hits the all-time low after the death of someone who has shared one's life so intimately. The feeling is physical. As though one's whole body has been chopped in two.

Your thoughts inevitably turn to Life after Death. Where has the spirit of your loved one gone? A shining vision of a glorious heavenly re-union (definite details unspecified) somehow does not fill the bill, but there is a faint underlying hope. Better to concentrate on the here and now, and take stock.

You have to come to terms with your ugly new title of Widow/Widower . . . a status in life you had never imagined yourself to be in. You are at rock bottom . . . you want to turn clocks back. All you want is to return to your comfortable and settled life of yesterday. It won't happen... you can never go back. This is the end of one of your "eras". Life will never be the same again. It has forced a U-turn on you.

Platitudes are showered upon you. You hear, times without number, that Time itself is a Great Healer. You can't believe it, but slowly the sharp edges of grief wear away, and you realise that one has to move on. The single state has its advantages. One has freedom to sort out a new life plan, explore new opportunities and meet new people. Easy to say, but it does need courage.

In old age, we have more years behind us than we have ahead, and thoughts of our own mortality become more persistent. We all hope that death will come to us suddenly, swiftly and painlessly, preferably in our own beds, without having to undergo the indignities of physical and mental deterioration. It rarely happens this way. Courage is what we need, and the faith and hope that God might be there at the end.

We hear more now about voluntary Euthanasia, which is unacceptable to most people, but welcomed by a few. Having lived in our bodies for X number of years, should we have the option of deciding when "enough is enough" while we are mentally able to make the decision?

For some people, it must be a great comfort and relief to escape the pain and indignity of a terminal illness, to accept death with courage and drink the fatal dose.

Do not go gentle into that good night,
Old age should burn and rave at close of day;
Rage, rage against the dying of the light.

~ Dylan Thomas

Attributions and Appreciations

The following friends and colleagues have generously contributed one or more pieces:

Bob Adams	Trevor Dealy	Ken Irvine	David Sayliss
Mary Allum	Wynford De La Haye	James Lamb	Phil Seager
Pam Booth	Mary Foster	Keith Levick	Ruth Skrine
Morag Bramley	Ian Gazzard	Lorna Macdougall	Mike Taylor
Paul Bramley	Janette Gazzard	Patricia Miles	John Tindall
John Britton	Michael Grafton	Pamela Paget	Jean Tyler
James Burton	Angela Grayson	Jean Penman	Eric Wilkes
Jane Cantrell	Derek Grayson	David Price	Carole Wilkinson
Ryland Clendon	Al Havenhand	Barrie Pursall	Ian Wordley
Malcolm Coackley	Maurice Hindle	Edna Pursall	

Acknowledgements

Most of the illustrations included in this book relate to some of the things people get up to in their retirement, whilst others have been selected purely because they are particularly beautiful, amusing, or interesting. The photographs have come from a number of different sources, and many of those eventually used are the work of James Kellie; the shot of *Mallard* on the Hope Valley line is by John Hilton.

The over-all design and layout of the book has been the skilled work of Peter Miles, upon whose experience we have leaned. Without him, there would have been no book.

David Price has acted as encourager and mentor throughout the project.

Permission to quote from the works of Carl Jung and T.S. Eliot has been granted by Harper Collins and Faber and Faber respectively.

The poems "An awakening" and "A change of view" were quoted by kind permission of the author Jean Tyler.

The book was compiled and edited by Paul Bramley with considerable support of those named and no doubt by others who have been regrettably forgotten. At 86 what can you expect?

Paul Bramley: *At various times and in sundry places most of Paul Bramley's working life was spent in the clinical practice and teaching of general medicine, dentistry and maxillofacial surgery. He was professor at Sheffield University for 20 years, Dean of Faculty at the Royal College of Surgeons of England, a Royal Commissioner, and a President of the B.D.A. The later burdens of Committee chairmanship were compensated by an increasing knowledge of the deviousness of human nature! 1984 saw him knighted. He never quite knew why.*

You know you're getting old when you go on holiday and always pack a sweater. ~ *Denis Norden*

Mallard passing through Hathersage on the Hope Valley Line

Life isn't measured by how many breaths we take, but by the moments that take our breath away.

~ Chinese saying